OAKWOOD LIBRARY OF RA

THE
SOUTH DEVON
RAILWAY

ROY GREGORY

THE OAKWOOD PRESS
1982

ACKNOWLEDGEMENTS

Without the co-operation of the staff of the local history department of the Plymouth City Library this work could not have materialised. Thanks go to them for their patience and help. Assistance has come from many other sources and in this context I would like to mention J. V. Somers-Cocks, Bernard Mills of the Plymouth Railway Circle, M. Williams of the Brunel Society, J. R. Pike, the South Devon Area Librarian and the staff at the Devon County Record Offices, Exeter and Plymouth, at the Public Record Office, Kew and at the National Railway Museum. Tribute must also be paid to Valerie Rendle for secretarial duties and the monumental task of typing the manuscript.

Cover drawing by Nicolas Trudgian:
South Devon Railway locomotive 'Etna'
passing Langstone Cliff Dawlish with a
Plymouth to Exeter train about 1874

ISBN 0 85361 286 2

CONTENTS

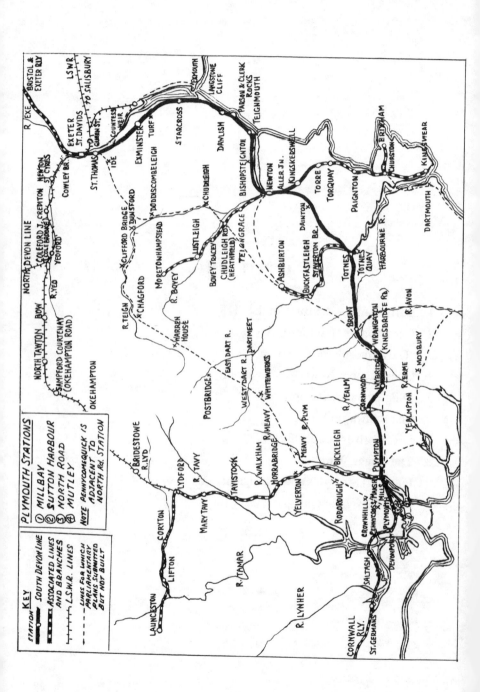

CHAPTER 1

EARLY PLANS — BIRTH OF THE SDR

Only a year after the Stockton & Darlington Railway was opened proposals were made to bring Plymouth on to the railway map. These were the first of several abortive schemes and a whole decade elapsed before there is evidence of any further positive move. The timing then was certainly propitious, because the Bristol & Exeter Railway obtained its Act on 19th May 1836 and a through line from London to Plymouth seemed feasible. During the summer of 1836 Brunel completed a survey for a route running from the proposed Bristol & Exeter Company's terminus at St. Davids, Exeter, to Plymouth via Dawlish, Teignmouth, Torquay, Dartmouth, Kingsbridge and Modbury. The rivers Teign and Dart would have been spanned by fairly lengthy bridges at Teignmouth and Dittisham respectively. Other expensive works were involved and the project had to be abandoned because finance was not forthcoming.

At about the same time Francis Giles, the engineer of the London & Southampton Railway, was considering a line via Crediton, Okehampton and Tavistock. For this he received support from Exonians, but none was forthcoming from the inhabitants of Plymouth, who wholeheartedly backed Brunel's line. Probably this is why, when the proposals for the London, Exeter & Falmouth Railway were deposited on 30th November 1836, no branch line to Plymouth was included.

Fresh proposals were put forward at a meeting held in Plymouth at the beginning of 1840. They were prepared by J.R. Rendel who had been apprenticed to Telford and who settled in Plymouth when appointed as engineer to the Plymouth & Dartmoor Railway. Rendel had three possible routes surveyed for a railway to Exeter:—

(1) A line approximately 64 miles long via the Tamar Valley, Launceston, Okehampton and Crediton.

(2) A southern route via Ivybridge, Totnes, Newton and Teignmouth which was slightly over 50 miles.

(3) What was described as the "direct route" across Dartmoor which cut the mileage to 37.

Telford himself made the first two surveys leaving the third to be carried out by his assistant N. Beardison. After considerable discussion a resolution was passed pledging strenuous support for the "direct" line. Since this included several extraordinary features it deserves a fairly detailed description.

It was to start at Pennycomequick, proceed up the Houndiscombe

Valley to Pennycross and thence to Crownhill, Yelverton, Meavy, Postbridge, Warren House, Chagford, Clifford Bridge, Dunsford, Ide and Exeter (St. Thomas). The first 1⅔ miles to Crownhill (then called Knackersknowle) had a gradient of 1 in 33 and was to be rope worked powered by two 60 H.P. stationary engines. Locomotives were then to be used to a point just beyond Meavy. Then came a very steep incline to be worked by rope and water wheel. This took the line up on to Dartmoor near Whiteworks at an elevation of 1,134 feet.

Two giant reservoirs were proposed near Princetown to ensure the supply of water. Locomotives would then have taken the trains to Warren House where the line had risen to a height of 1,190 feet. There was to be a tunnel at each end of this section, one 1,300 yards long at the Whiteworks end and the other, 1,760 yards in length, at Warren House. From this point the line would have descended to the Teign Valley near Chagford and here there was to be another incline worked by rope and water wheel. Two more reservoirs were proposed nearby, one in the East Dart Valley and the other made by damming the Stats Brook. From the foot of this second incline to Exeter locomotives would have been used again.

The estimated cost was put at £770,781 to include a branch line from Yelverton to Tavistock. This, it was claimed, would represent a saving of more than a million pounds compared with the southern route and operating costs would be materially lower. Obviously it was this alleged cost saving which influenced those who backed this scheme which, viewed in retrospect, seems so fantastic. In fact, however, a provisional committee was set up, a Parliamentary Bill deposited on 29th February 1840 and £62,000 capital subscribed. Enthusiasm for this project waned however as doubts were expressed about the viability of a railway traversing so much wasteland.

Meanwhile considerable pressure was being built up by the business fraternity in Plymouth who were anxious to get the town connected to the rapidly expanding railway network. Attention became diverted to Rendel's route to the south of Dartmoor and in October 1842 another public meeting was held. Its purpose was to test attitudes of local inhabitants and landowners whose property would be affected and in particular to see what financial support would be forthcoming. One fact which did emerge was that there was little hope of raising the required capital entirely from local resources.

At this stage however the exact route to be followed was still not finally decided. A.J. Rhodes mentions that a line passing through Ashburton and Chudleigh was proposed as an alternative to Rendel's route through Newton. He then went on to give details of a census which was taken to decide whether Ashburton or Newton would be likely to generate the most traffic. Men were stationed for three weeks by the clock tower in Newton and at the centre of Ashburton to count and record the number of people entering and leaving each town. At Ashburton interested parties ran cabs in and out of the town offering free rides to travellers with the object of increasing the flow of traffic. Despite this ruse however the figures for Newton vastly exceeded those for Ashburton. Furthermore, Teignmouth and Torquay could be served more conveniently by a route passing through Newton.

There was also considerable argument in Plymouth about the site of the terminus. Support from the citizens of Devonport was only obtained on the promise of a station near the north east barrier gate which was at the east end of Fore Street fairly close to where the London & South Western Company's King's Road station was built many years later.

Brunel's recommendation was that the terminus should be at Eldad. Whilst this would not have honoured the agreement regarding Devonport it was eminently suited for an extension to that town and on to Cornwall. When this site was initially chosen it came in for strong criticism however. One local dignitary, George Soltau, dubbed Brunel's choice "No Place" and alleged that passengers alighting there would be as likely to find their way to Devonport as to Plymouth. He had advocated a terminus at Friary, but this too was ridiculed by other people, including Brunel, because it was at one extrimity of the "three towns" of Plymouth, Stonehouse and Devonport.

Incidentally, there is a hostelry called the "No Place Inn" near the top of the old Eldad Hill. Although other explanations have been put forward for the derivation of this title it is interesting to speculate that it could well have resulted from Soltau's description of the site.

At the other end of the line the inhabitants of Exeter continued their hostility and organised a deprecatory campaign. They feared the loss of considerable trade to Plymouth because of the better port facilities which it could offer. This was of course one of the points being canvasssed by the promoters of the new railway.

Despite the arguments and disagreements the forces for progress prevailed and it was not long before this was demonstrated in a practical way. The Associated Companies' broad gauge lines were sweeping steadily westward having reached Taunton on 1st July 1842 and Beam Bridge, beyond Wellington, on 1st May 1843. Before long they would extend to Exeter. It seemed logical, therefore, that they would now be interested in what was being done about the construction of a railway beyond Exeter to Plymouth, and so it turned out to be. They were persuaded to come forward with financial support for the project and an agreement was thrashed out, the principal conditions being:—

(1) That the coastal line selected by Messrs. Brunel and Rendel be

adopted and that it be carried to a point between Plymouth and Devonport which would be most convenient for an extension into Cornwall.

(2) That the Associated Companies should have the right to appoint eight out of the fifteen directors of the Plymouth, Devonport & Exeter Railway Company.

(3) That £500,000 towards the capital required should be subscribed from other (local) sources before the Associated Companies were to incur any payment, deposit or other liability and before a Parliamentary Act was sought.

Support for this agreement was pledged at meetings which were held in October 1843, the first at Newton chaired by the Earl of Devon and the second at Plymouth at which the Mayor, W. Prance, presided. It was not until then that the provisional committee which had been set up in 1840 finally decided to abandon the proposals for the direct line across Dartmoor.

During the same month a prospectus was issued which detailed a route starting from the Bristol & Exeter Company's terminus at Exeter St. David's and terminating at Eldad, Plymouth, a total distance of 51½ miles. The actual route will be described later. It was broadly the same as that followed by the existing main line from Exeter to the site of the present Plymouth station. The principal variations were:—

(1) Between Langstone Cliff (by Dawlish Warren) and Teignmouth where, at the behest of the Admiralty engineer, the line had to be brought closer to the cliffs than Brunel had intended.

(2) At Newton Abbot where there was a public protest when it was discovered that the line would barely enter the parish and that the proposed station would be 500 yards to the west of Forde House. The inhabitants threatened opposition to the Bill in the House of Lords and to avoid this a diversion was agreed. Instead of the line running direct from Hackney to Forde House a loop was made increasing the overall distance by roughly half a mile.

(3) At various points over the hilly terrain between Newton and Plymouth where gradients were increased and the radius of some curves reduced.

Provision was included for a branch to the waterside at or near Millbay, Plymouth, from which locomotives were banned if Stonehouse Lane, Union Street and/or Millbay Road was crossed on the level. Also, powers were included to acquire or lease all or part of the Plymouth & Dartmoor Railway and to extend it along the shores of the Cattewater and Sutton Harbour at Plymouth. A further clause authorised the acquisition of the ferry which operated between Exmouth and Dawlish Warren. Intermediate stations were to be built at Exeter (St. Thomas), Starcross, Dawlish, Teignmouth, Newton, Totnes,

South Brent, Wrangaton, Ivybridge and Plympton and arrangements were to be provided for the joint use, with the Bristol & Exeter Company, of St. David's station.

Soon afterwards the Company's name was changed to the South Devon Railway Company and on 1st November it was announced that the Parliamentary Bill would be deposited in the next session. Fortunately no rival scheme was put forward and few difficulties were encountered in the promotion and passage of the Bill. The Company received its Act on 4th July 1844. One new section was inserted which made Admiralty approval necessary for all the works along the banks of the River Exe, those fronting the coast thence to Teignmouth and also those on the estuary of the River Plym at Laira.

The authorised share capital was fixed at £1,100,000 divided into shares of £50 each and the Associated Companies agreed to subscribe for shares to a nominal value of £400,000 made up as follows:—

Great Western Railway £150,000
Bristol & Exeter Railway £200,000
Bristol & Gloucester Railway.... £ 50,000

The number of directors was increased to 21 of whom 11 were to be nominated by these three companies and the remaining 10 by other subscribers. It was agreed that the Chairman and his deputy should be elected from those representing the other subscribers but by virtue of numerical strength the Associated Companies were in a position to exercise overall control.

Little time was lost before calling the first General Meeting of members, held at the Royal Hotel, Plymouth, on 28th August 1844 under the chairmanship of Thomas Gill, M.P., a prominent local businessman. The Chairman emphasised that the route now chosen was considered to be far more advantageous than the others projected so that shareholders would be more than compensated for the cost of the surveys. The investigation into the traffic potential as proved before the Parliamentary Committee was highly satisfactory, and in this context traffic on the Bristol & Exeter line had already exceeded expectations. He went on to say that another matter which might excite and surprise those present was the decision of the Directors to adopt the Atmospheric System of propulsion. Since the Act was passed the Directors had been approached by the Samuda Brothers, the patentees, who claimed that their system was particularly suited to the proposed line and would have many advantages over locomotive working. Mr Brunel, the Engineer, was consulted and he decided to arrange for some Directors to visit Ireland to see it in action. Mr Brunel was decidedly in favour of the system and this view was shared by the Directors so the Board had therefore decided to adopt it. The Chairman admitted that at first he thought it unwise to use it, believing

.it it was unsuited to the particular circumstances of this neighbourhood, but after witnessing what he did on the Dublin & Dalkey Railway his prejudices were entirely removed.

Needless to say, considerable discussion followed this momentous announcement. Upon ascertaining that only the section from Kingstown to Dalkey, a distance of 1¾ miles, was atmospherically worked, one shareholder pointed out that there was a vast difference between operating a line of this length and one exceeding 50 miles. Brunel replied that this had been carefully considered and had they not been satisfied that it could be applied as well to 50 miles as to 1¾ miles the Directors would not have recommended it. Other questions were raised concerning difficulties in crossing trains, speed and economy of working. Brunel, dealing with the first point, replied that it would cause no problem, and the Chairman added that whilst 45 miles per hour was the ordinary rate of travelling on the Dalkey line, he did not doubt that much higher speeds would be possible over the longer stretches of this line. Furthermore, lower operating costs could be anticipated if this system was employed.

When the resolution to adopt atmospheric working was finally put to the meeting it was carried without dissent. So the scene was set for what was later to be described by the local inhabitants as the "Atmospheric Caper" — but that is a story in itself.

Before starting the story of its construction it will help to complete the picture by describing the salient features of the railway and the territory through which it was built. For this the line can conveniently be split into two sections, the first covering the twenty miles from Exeter to Newton which was comparatively flat, and the second dealing with the decidedly hilly terrain which had to be traversed thence to Plymouth.

The River Exe is crossed immediately on leaving St. David's Station and embankments and arches carry the line for nearly a mile to St. Thomas. The Cathedral can be seen high on the left. Soon the line runs close to the Exeter Canal, still used by large vessels which sometimes give the impression when viewed from a passing train that they are steaming up through meadows grazed by cattle and sheep. After passing Exminster (5m) Turf is reached which marks the end of the canal. The west bank of the River Exe is then followed passing the Earl of Devon's Castle at Powderham with its deer park and then on through Starcross (8½m) to Dawlish Warren (10½m). Here the rails run past Langstone Cliff and are then laid on a ledge cut out from the cliff face as far as Dawlish (12m). Between Dawlish and Teignmouth (15m) this ledge is continued but it is interspersed by a tunnel through each of the five intervening headlands. There was a sixth tunnel, since opened out, shortly before reaching Teignmouth Station.

An interesting story is told by a local historian concerning the "Parson and Clerk" rocks, well known landmarks seen to the east of Teignmouth. He alleges that the original rocks which bore these titles were further out to sea. The old "Parson" collapsed during a gale but the local inhabitants, determined not to be deprived of their ecclesiastical friends, ordained the present rocks with the titles.

From Teignmouth the north bank of the Teign estuary is followed until the railway crosses that river and the Stover Canal by a bridge near Newton Station (20m).

Having followed river banks and the open sea the line now veers inland to Aller which lies at the foot of a steep bank rising to Dainton Tunnel (24m). This unbroken climb of nearly 2½ miles has a maximum gradient of 1 in 37. Next comes the descent to Totnes (29m) but speed has to be kept in check because of the tight curves as the line follows the contours of the rounded hills. The River Dart is bridged immediately before arriving at Totnes Station. Rattery Bank, considerably longer but not quite as steep as Dainton, begins at once. Soon after crossing the Harbourne River on a short viaduct the single-bore Marley Tunnel is reached. The climb continues to Brent (36m) where there is a bridge over the River Avon, past Glaze viaduct and on to Wrangaton (38m). Here the line attains its highest altitude having risen 442 feet in a distance of slightly under 9 miles from Totnes, the average gradient being 1 in 107 with a maximum, near the commencement, of 1 in 48.

Now the railway skirts the southern slopes of Dartmoor giving panoramic views over the South Hams country and spanning four more river valleys on viaducts at Bittaford (39m), Ivybridge (41½m), Blachford and Slade. At Hemerdon (45½m) the high ground is left behind and the steep descent to Plympton (48m) starts. This bank, which is nearly 2½ miles long, has an average gradient of 1 in 42 and brings the railway down almost to sea level once again. The River Plym is crossed at Marsh Mills and its estuary is followed as far as Laira. Then comes the climb to Mutley Tunnel — the last major civil engineering work before the Plymouth terminus is reached (52¾m).

NOTE: Figures in brackets denote approximate distances from St. David's.

CHAPTER 2

CONSTRUCTION — EXETER TO NEWTON

Initially, construction was concentrated mainly on the section from Exeter to Newton. This was slightly over twenty miles and roughly two-fifths of the total length of the line. It will be observed that the station to serve both Newton Abbot and Newton Bushel was tactfully named "Newton", the "Abbot" not being added until 1877 to distinguish it from other Newtons.

In accordance with the Director's decision, endorsed at the first shareholders meeting on 28th August 1844, a single broad gauge line was to be laid throughout, with passing places. The track was of bridge rails fixed on to longitudinal timbers and was laid throughout on a bed of shale. The use of this material for the track bed was far from satisfactory and it was not long before it had to be replaced by broken stone and gravel.

The principal works comprised:—

(1) A timber bridge over the River Exe immediately to the west of the terminus at Exeter.

(2) A viaduct of 62 arches to carry the line over the St. Thomas District of Exeter.

(3) A river wall along the west bank of the Exe estuary between Powderham and the Warren at Dawlish.

(4) An embankment across Cockwood Marsh to the south of Starcross.

(5) Removing a massive quantity of rock from the cliff-face between Dawlish Warren and Teignmouth to form the ledge on which the permanent way was to be laid.

(6) Building a sea wall and groins to protect the line along this section.

(7) Boring six tunnels between Dawlish and Teignmouth: Kennaway (210 yards), Coryton (230 yards), Phillot (50 yards), Clerk's (60 yards), Parson's (370 yards), East Teignmouth (320 yards).

(8) Two covered ways, one on each side of Teignmouth Station.

(9) An embankment at the approach to Newton and a bridge to carry the track over the River Teign and the entrance to the Stover Canal.

It will be observed that the embankment across Cockwood Marsh did not materialise. For the record, the tunnel at East Teignmouth was opened out when the line was doubled between Dawlish Station and Teignmouth Old Quay. It is assumed that the two covered ways were abolished at the same time. The one at the east of the station was quite short but the other was about 300 yards long commencing near milepost 209. These works at Teignmouth and Dawlish were undertaken by the G.W.R. between 1879 and 1884.

Reverting to the original construction, quite good progress had been made by February 1845. The viaduct at St. Thomas was almost complete and the track-bed prepared as far as Powderham. On the coastal stretch however the weather had already begun to play its part. There was an exceptional prevalence of easterly winds during the winter which had seriously delayed landing the stone for the sea wall. This material was being brought to the site by sea in skips. Nevertheless, a considerable length of the sea wall was complete, tunnelling was proceeding satisfactorily between Dawlish and Teignmouth and cutting out a terrace for the line at the foot of the cliffs was going forward fairly well. This was an operation which required considerable heavy blasting.

Doubts continued to be expressed in some quarters about the safety of a line laid in such an exposed position, but Brunel had no misgivings. He pointed out that the wall where completed had stood up perfectly to battering from several severe gales. The only damage done had been at Langstone Cliff where heavy seas had scoured away the beach. This had only happened because the mortar was still soft and the wall had been forced out by pressure from behind. This damage he asserted would not have occurred had the groins been in position at the time. Furthermore, he thought that very little of the line would eventually be reached by the highest tides.

At the Teignmouth end the tunnel through the Parson's Rock headland was three-quarters completed, but very little had been done beyond this point in the vicinity of Teignmouth. This was because negotiations with the Harbour Commissioners there could not be finalised. The contract date for the completion of the work fronting the sea shore between Langstone Rock and Teignmouth was 1st June 1845 and with his usual optimism Brunel did not doubt that it would be completed on schedule, despite the fact that only about three more months remained when this forecast was made.

Not only did the contractors fail to attain their target date for the sea-shore works — there were other difficulties with the result that no part of the line could be opened for traffic until twelve months afterwards. One of the major problems proved to be the crossing of Cockwood Marsh, once described as "an unfathomable mire", a title fully justified by events. It proved to be so deep that the idea of an embankment had to be abandoned and in its place Brunel designed a 200 yard viaduct to carry the line across.

Two statements were made at the half-yearly meeting held in March

1846. The first, made by Brunel, was as usual very reassuring. He said that he had personally inspected all the works and was entirely satisfied that both the route and the mode of traction would prove to be perfectly safe, convenient and agreeable for the public. Afterwards the Chairman announced that the line from Exeter to Teignmouth was virtually complete except for laying the atmospheric tubing. The Directors had therefore decided to open this section of the line in the spring by using locomotives, without waiting for the atmospheric installations to be completed. They hoped very soon afterwards to extend operations to within half a mile of Newton.

The reasoning seemed straightforward: the line was almost ready for use apart from the atmospheric apparatus, so it was only right that the public should benefit by having a train service as soon as possible. However, the real reason behind this move was no doubt to raise some revenue as soon as possible to relieve the financial pressures which were building up.

Arrangements were quickly concluded with the G.W.R. for hiring two engines. Both were of the 2-2-2 class and they were specially renamed "Exe" and "Teign". The hire charge was to be 1s/4d (approx 7p) per train mile.

The service was advertised to commence on Whit-Saturday, 30th May 1846 and by good fortune the weather was perfect. The first train left Exeter at 12.25 p.m. and comprised nine carriages hauled by "Teign". Free tickets had been issued to shareholders for this inaugural run. There were three intermediate stations, at Exeter St. Thomas, Starcross and Dawlish, and large crowds had assembled all along the route to witness the spectacle and to cheer the train on its way. Upon arrival at Teignmouth a band played "See the Conquering Hero Comes", flags were hoisted by the ships in the harbour and the whole town presented what was described as "a scene of indescribable gaiety and delight". At 1.27 p.m. the train set off on its return journey to Exeter which was reached 38 minutes later.

Traffic built up over this bank holiday week-end beyond the wildest dreams of the Directors and others concerned with the Railway. The Exeter "Flying Post" reported that, following the heavy traffic on Whit Sunday, all was surpassed on the Monday when from 7 o'clock in the morning onwards Exonians swarmed to their two stations for a trip to the sea. Twenty-one carriages were put on the morning train which conveyed an estimated 1,500 passengers and, surprisingly, about an equal number turned up to travel on the corresponding Up train.

Completion of the line into Newton was delayed until Parliamentary powers were obtained enabling the Company to acquire one parcel of land and so overcome the difficulties which had arisen. An earlier intention to operate to within about half a mile of that town until this obstacle could be by-passed was evidently abandoned because of difficulty of access to the town from a temporary terminus. Possession of the land required was not obtained until the late summer and then a start had to be made on the earthworks necessary at that point. Furthermore work had not been pressed forward on the bridges to span the River Teign and the Canal or on the station site because the question of a possible deviation was involved. These heavy works were tackled at once, and before the end of December the line was ready for traffic.

The first test train entered Newton Station on Tuesday, 22nd December 1846. It comprised two locomotives hauling a large number of trucks loaded with between 300 and 400 tons deadweight. The local press reported that the bridges bore this enormous load without any apparent vibration and the embankment, which many thought could never be negotiated, bore the strain without showing the slightest tendency to sink! On Monday, 28th December, the line was surveyed by the Government Inspector, Captain Coddington, and he pronounced it to be entirely satisfactory. Three days later, on 31st December, this part of the line was opened for passenger traffic. The first through train hauled by the "Sun" Class locomotive "Antelope" left Exeter at 9.55 a.m. and arrived at Newton at 10.45 a.m. On the opening day five trains ran in each direction but subsequently the week-day service comprised six trains each way, with three in each direction on Sundays. All the trains were hauled by locomotives because the atmospheric installations were still not ready.

Celebrations to mark the arrival of the railway at Newton were strangely lacking, a paradoxical situation bearing in mind how much the town was to owe to the railway for its future prosperity.

CHAPTER 3

'THE ATMOSPHERIC CAPER'

Having followed the construction and opening of the line as far as Newton this seems to be the appropriate time to consider the atmospheric episode. Initially it is important to review the historical background and, without too much technical detail, to see broadly how the system worked.

The firm of Samuda & Clegg patented in 1839 a method of harnessing the atmospheric pressure and utilising it for traction. This had aroused very considerable interest in the railway world and had not only been adopted by the London & Croydon Railway but was actually working on the Kingstown & Dalkey line in Ireland when the South Devon Railway first became involved. One can say that a "minimania" in atmospheric railways was beginning to develop. Various projects were promoted including direct lines between London and Liverpool, Manchester and Portsmouth and also such schemes as the Great Eastern & Western from Yarmouth to Swansea and Cooke's National Railway with a multitude of lines including London to Edinburgh, London to Exeter, etc. etc.

Brunel, for his part, was looking for some form of supplementary power, being convinced that the unavoidably steep gradients between Newton and Plymouth would be too heavy to be worked by locomotives unaided. Another vital aspect concerned finance. Although the Railway was backed by the G.W.R., the B. & E. and the Bristol and Gloucester Companies, money was not likely to come in too liberally from local subscribers so the Board was anxious to keep the cost of construction down as much as possible. They were in fact after a railway "on the cheap".

Such then was the position when in July 1844, immediately after the South Devon's Parliamentary Act had been obtained, Messrs. Samuda & Clegg contacted the Board and suggested that their system of propulsion be adopted, arguing that it was eminently suitable to cope with the heavy gradients beyond Newton. Shortly afterwards Thomas Gill, the Chairman, and several officers of the Company visited the Kingstown & Dalkey line and were so impressed with what they saw that they asked Brunel to make a full report on the possibilities for adopting the atmospheric system on their railway.

Brunel was not the only celebrated engineer to visit the Dalkey line for Daniel Gooch and Robert Stephenson also made the pilgrimage. Gooch was not at all impressed and tried to dissuade Brunel from adopting it. He was concerned about the immense cost and did not accept the claims made that the operating cost was only 7d (approx. 3p) per mile compared with 1/4d (approx. 7p) per mile on the locomotive-hauled section of the Dublin & Kingstown Railway. Robert Stephenson regarded atmospheric working with even greater disfavour. His principal objection was also on the grounds of cost and he could not accept Samuda's claim that as much traffic could be carried on a single line operated atmospherically as on a double track with locomotives. He also noted that there were mechanical difficulties which could be aggravated as traffic grew.

Brunel, however, was not influenced by the views of these eminent engineers. Whilst well aware of the shortcomings on the Dalkey line he was confident that they could be overcome. Not surprisingly, therefore, when Brunel made his report to the directors on 19th August 1844 it favoured atmospheric traction on the South Devon Railway. In the report he made the following points:—

(1) An important cost saving could result from laying a single track with passing places in lieu of a double track throughout. Also, without locomotives he could make some further economies by reducing the radius of curves and by increasing some gradients. The total savings in capital outlay were estimated to be £257,000, offset by the cost of atmospheric installations totalling £190,000, producing a net saving of £67,000. Furthermore he anticipated annual operating costs would be reduced by £8,000.

(2) Stationary power if freed from weight and friction of any material such as rope would, apart from producing cheaper motive power, also be more in command and capable of much higher speeds than locomotives. He considered that speeds of at least 60 miles per hour were possible. If locomotives were used on this line he thought that the weight of the engine and tender could not be much less than half the gross weight of the train.

(3) The mechanical difficulties on the Dalkey line which had worried Robert Stephenson could be overcome so that the full degree of vacuum produced by pumping could be transmitted to a piston on a train without material loss or friction.

(4) Frequent services could be provided which would be free of noise and dirt.

(5) Collisions would be impossible because only one train could occupy each section at a time.

To sum up, he considered that the atmospheric system was an effective means of working trains by stationary power whether over long or short lines, at higher speeds and with less risk than could be achieved with locomotives.

Brunel could well claim speeds of 60 miles per hour in the light of an event on the Dalkey line where an engineering student named Frank

Elrington was probably the first man in the world to travel at 100 m.p.h. Due to a misunderstanding whilst preparations were being made for a test run the piston carriage in which he was seated was propelled forward before being coupled to the train. The ascent was made at an average speed of 84 m.p.h., so that the maximum attained must have been well in excess of this figure!

The directors accepted Brunel's report and an agreement was negotiated with Samuda & Clegg; orders were placed with Messrs. Boulton & Watt, Rennies and Maudsley & Field for the engine house machinery and equipment.

Having reached the stage where the final decision had been made it is opportune to examine the basic principles of the system. A continuous length of cast iron tube which was slotted at the top was laid between the running rails. Hinged to one side of the slot was a flap or valve made of ox-hide leather reinforced with iron plates which could be sealed by use of a special composition, lime soap being used originally. At the head of the train was a special vehicle called a piston carriage. As its name implies it carried a piston which fitted into the continuous tube and was connected by a bar fitted with a universal joint to the underside of the carriage. This bar was known as a coulter. A pin which held the coulter was designed so that it would break if the piston hit any obstruction. Thus the coulter and piston would be left behind as the train proceeded on its way. The piston was approximately 15 feet long and shaped somewhat like a dumbbell. The piston head which was leather covered protruded forward from the coulter joint and was balanced by a lead counterweight to the rear of that joint. Behind the piston head and mounted on the top of the rod which held it were two wheels which pressed open the valve on the continuous pipe, one section at a time, after the piston had passed ahead. This admitted air so enabling the piston to be pushed forward by atmospheric pressure. Behind the coulter were two more wheels to take the weight of the valve until it dropped back into the closed position. Finally, a spring wheel on the underside of the piston carriage pressed the valve flap firmly back into its slot, so sealing the tube in readiness for the re-creation of the vacuum for the next train.

At terminals the piston had to be taken out of the pipe so that the carriage could be turned. At times the piston carriage could stop at a point where the piston was not in the continuous pipe — e.g. at a junction, passing place or siding. To cope with such a situation a small 8" supplementary pipe was fitted beside the nearside rail. This supplementary pipe was connected to the main pipe ahead. A rope was then connected between a piston in this small tube and a bar on the piston carriage. This developed sufficient power to move the train or carriage forward to the point where the piston could enter the main tube. Occasionally the rope broke and this caused at least one fatality. At junctions and crossovers there had to be a break in the continuous tube so that it would not foul the crossing rails. The ends were sealed by self acting valves and the piston could leave one section of tube and enter the next whilst the train was in motion; the maximum speed at which this could safely be done does not seem to have been recorded. A subsidiary by-pass tube below rail level joined the two sections of the main tube. A break was also required at each engine house. Here the same self-acting valves were used on the main tube but there was a complicated subsidiary system of tubes and cut-off valves by which:—

(1) Any one section could be pumped by the engines at either end of the length.

(2) Any intermediate engine house could pump simultaneously from the lengths at each side.

(3) More than one length could be joined and pumped from one station. From a practical point of view the limit was probably two lengths — i.e. 6 miles.

Also at junctions, crossovers and other obstructions a ramp was provided to lift the piston clear. Braking had to be restricted to handbrakes fitted to the piston carraige and in the guard's compartment. Since the brakes had to operate against the atmospheric pressure pushing the piston forward trains often overshot the station platforms. Capstans were installed in places for use when shunting. Theoretically the effectiveness of the system depended upon the diameter of the tube and the degree of vacuum created by the pumps. In practice other factors impaired efficiency.

Originally Brunel ordered main tubes 13″ in diameter for the first section of line between Exeter and Newton, intending to increase the diameter to 22″ on the South Devon banks and to 15″ on the remainder of the line from Newton to Plymouth and to Torquay. To make this a practical proposition he had invented a piston capable of being expanded or contracted in diameter. The main tube was manufactured in 10 foot lengths with a 2½″ slot at the top. This produced the first of many snags which were to be encountered, since, because of the slot, it was not originally possible to produce tubes entirely free of distortion. However T.R. Guppy evolved an effective casting procedure to overcome this technical problem and then the tube was manufactured at a rate of about 500 lengths a week.

Soon however, Brunel decided that in the light of experience on the Croydon line (which had opened in January 1845) the 13″ tube was unlikely to produce the power which would be needed. After 4,400 tons of it had been produced he changed his mind and ordered 15″ tubes instead for the original section. By Christmas 1845 it was possible to make a start on assembling the continuous tube. The sections were socketed and the joints filled with a mixture of oil and wax kept in place by hemp cord saturated in pitch and hammered in to make the joints airtight.

As assembly took place the inside surface of the tube was given a thin coating of tallow so as to produce a polished friction free surface for the passage of the piston.

The Railway Chronicle dated 11th April 1846 stated that between 7 and 8 miles of tubing had then been laid and caulked and that in all 16 miles of tubing had been delivered from foundries at Bridgewater and Bristol. By the late spring the tube had been continued as far as Dawlish but its installation beyond that point was considerably delayed. Materials for the main valve were also delivered, but for some reason none appears to have been fitted to the tube. Had this been done as the tube was assembled it would have given protection from dirt and the weather to the polished inside surface and some of the subsequent difficulties may have been eased or even avoided altogether.

Work was also proceeding on the engine houses which were built to an ornate exterior design by Brunel. It was decided to site these at intervals of roughly three miles, and they were erected at Exeter, Countess Weir, Turf, Starcross, Dawlish, Teignmouth, Bishopsteignton and Newton. Each engine house contained an engine room with two large 41½ h.p. vertical engines with cylinders of 33″ bore and 72″ stroke. These engines could be worked either independently or linked. Each engine was designed to drive an air pump with cylinders of 33″ bore and 72″ stroke which sucked air from the tube to create the vacuum. There were also two small donkey engines which worked the boiler feed pumps and coal-lifting cranes. Also the engine houses contained a boiler room, coal store, general store and water tank. Adjacent were coal sidings and a reservoir.

In the spring of 1846 the first two engines were delivered by Messrs. Boulton & Watt of Soho and installed at Exeter. These were followed by engines for Turf and Starcross from the same manufacturers. Messrs. Rennie supplied the engines for Countess Weir, Teignmouth and Newton and Messrs. Maudsley were the suppliers for Dawlish and Bishopsteignton. By August at least one engine had been tested and by February 1847 their installation had been completed as far as Dawlish.

On 25th February 1847 the first piston carriage was delivered and no time was lost in putting it to the test since a trial run was made as far as Turf that very evening. The resident engineer, P.J. Margery, made the following entry in his journal — "Started at 6 p.m. for Turf towing a locomotive behind. Went on very slowly to Turf there being a large quantity of water and dirt in the pipe".

The following day Messrs. Samuda and Brunel made their first atmospheric trip on the line in a light train of only two carriages. At the shareholders meeting shortly afterwards Samuda reported that all had gone well, adding that within a fortnight atmospheric working would be extended experimentally as far as Dawlish, but this was clearly soft-soap for the shareholders who were by then getting very restive about the continuing delays. Incidentally, on each of these two occasions a 6 mile pull was taken because the intermediate station at Countess Weir had not been brought into operation. Despite this, a considerable speed was claimed for part of the journey on the second day.

In the course of subsequent trials there were so many troubles that it was clear that an early service to the public was out of the question. The stationary engines got off to a very bad start, there being several breakdowns including broken cranks and couplings. Furthermore some of the engines ran extremely roughly. The causes were a combination of underpowered engines and poor workmanship and many modifications were required, all adding to the existing delays.

There were also troubles with the valve and the directors' anxieties were doubtless increased when they learned that the Board of the London & Croydon Railway had decided to abandon atmospheric working on 4th May 1847. Samuda continued to make reassuring statements however, this time promising atmospheric working as far as Teignmouth by the middle of June. This proved to be another wildly optimistic forecast for it was not until 16th August that the first atmospheric train reached that town.

Thereafter experimental atmospheric trains were run daily between Exeter and Teignmouth. Down trains left Exeter at 3 p.m. and 6.30 p.m. whilst Up trains departed from Teignmouth at 10.45 a.m. and 4 p.m. The journey time was scheduled at 40 minutes and intermediate stops were made at Starcross and Dawlish. No passengers were allowed to travel on these trains. Generally speeds of up to 45 m.p.h. were attained but at times this speed was exceeded. The 'Plymouth, Devonport & Stonehouse Herald' reported very favourably stating that every experiment proved to be successful. Trains were stated to have been thoroughly under control stopping at stations with perfect precision even when heavily loaded. On the second day (Tuesday) a train comprising four carriages conveying friends of the engineers together with three trucks loaded with coal was described as having travelled from Exeter to Teignmouth at a terrific pace. On the Wednesday a trial run was made with a goods train of eleven trucks loaded to 120 tons. It covered the 8¼ miles from Exeter to Starcross in 15 minutes. The reporter concluded by saying that "the happy and successful results of the past week must have dispelled any remaining doubts about the practicability of this superior mode of traction". Despite this glowing tribute however all was not going well.

News of the atmospheric operations naturally spread rapidly around the railway world, so that when the half-yearly meeting of the Company was held at the Royal Hotel, Plymouth, on 28th August, several of the great railway celebrities of the time were there. The presence of Robert Stephenson, who might well be described as the arch-critic of atmospheric railways and George Hudson, M.P., Chairman of the Midland line and known as "The Railway King", must have made Brunel bitterly disappointed at being unable to announce the early introduction of atmospheric service trains. However, Mr Gill the Chairman was cheered when he said that nothing had happened to reduce his faith in the atmospheric system. The meeting was then addressed by George Hudson, who said that he had been over the whole line and saw its capabilities. He was convinced that, managed with economy and judgment, it could pay its way and earn a fair dividend for shareholders. It was not, however, a line capable of absorbing much by way of experimental projects and he had therefore felt obliged, both personally and on behalf of the Midland Railway, to obtain from the Chairman a pledge that no more should be done in connection with atmospheric installations beyond Totnes until the system had been fully tested over the section up to that town. Despite this pledge however the directors did decide later to make provision for such installations to provide supplementary power on the Rattery and Hemerdon banks.

A matter which was causing immediate concern to the directors at the time was Brunel's failure to conclude any contracts for engine houses and their machinery between Newton and Totnes. There was however good reason for this delay. The original 41½ h.p. engines had been ordered to work pumps to extract air from a 13″ tube. A 15″ tube had been substituted and the machinery was clearly being heavily taxed even on the level section for all but the lightest trains. Brunel had decided to use a 22″ pipe over the whole distance beyond Newton where there were heavy gradients to be negotiated. He was therefore anxious to accumulate as much practical experience as possible before deciding the capacity of the engines and pumps required. He later decided upon 68 h.p. horizontal engines of an improved design. Meantime the valves on the Boulton & Watt engines were replaced and other modifications made resulting in much improved operation despite having to be driven hard to compensate for the inadequate pumps.

Early in September a daily goods train was regularly transferred to atmospheric working and the great day when the public could sample it for the first time was Monday, 13th September. From that date two daily atmospheric service trains were run in each direction. The Up trains left Teignmouth at 10.45 a.m. and 4 p.m. as the experimental ones had done but the Down trains were re-timed to leave Exeter at 2.50 p.m. and 6.30 p.m.

Testing was continued in order to establish the full operational potential of the system. With a train of 28 tons a maximum speed of 68 m.p.h. was attained with an average speed of 64 m.p.h. over three level miles. With the train load increased to 100 tons however, the maximum speed reached was only 35 m.p.h.

Additional trains were soon transferred from locomotive working, evidenced by an article in "Besley's Chronicle" concerning a journey from Exeter to Teignmouth on Saturday, 25th September, by what the reporter described as "the much abused atmospheric power of propulsion". The train, the 9.50 a.m. from Exeter, comprised five carriages and was timed over the three miles between the engine houses at Countess Weir and Turf. This distance was covered in 2 minutes 50 seconds giving an average speed exceeding 60 m.p.h. The trip was described as virtually free from noise and so smooth that it was possible to write with ease whilst travelling at between 40 and 50 m.p.h. On the same day Brunel and Samuda made a non-stop test run from Exeter St. Thomas to Teignmouth covering the 14¼ miles in 17 minutes to give an average speed slightly exceeding 50 m.p.h.

On 17th December further services were transferred to the atmospheric system including the daily express in each direction and some service trains were worked for the first time by this method as far as Newton. By 10th January 1848 the majority of the trains between Exeter and Newton were using the new system and on 23rd February the changeover was complete.

The new method of propulsion appeared to be working very well and a lot of favourable comment was made, it being described as singularly smooth and agreeable and freed from the annoyance of coke dust and fumes. So, it seemed, all was set fair for Brunel's latest engineering experiment and it appeared that the great man's reputation could be enhanced rather than impaired despite the cruel criticism which had been meted out to him from some sources.

Although all trains between Newton and Exeter were now being atmospherically hauled this situation was only achieved with considerable difficulty and expense. Within two months from the public opening of the atmospheric service the longitudinal valve was giving trouble which led to the constant employment of a gang of men to keep it well greased so as to minimise the effect of leakages. The leaks were causing a lot of trouble and it was taking far longer than Brunel's estimate of from three to five minutes to exhaust air from the three-mile sections and the pumping effort had to be increased by anything up to three times the anticipated figure. Rain water was getting into the tube and it was sometimes necessary to run a piston carriage throughout the length to clear the nightly accumulation as a prelude to commencing the daily service.

Whilst the telegraph was installed at stations it had not been laid on to the engine houses where it was most needed for economical working. Engines and pumps were therefore worked according to the time-tables which led to them being overworked, and resulted with the other factors mentioned in very inflated fuel bills. On top of these troubles Devon suffered a spell of severely cold weather between December 1847 and February 1848 and the valve became frozen fairly frequently. On a few occasions it was necessary to bring in locomotives for assistance, but only on one day, 10th January, when a sudden severe frost occurred quite unexpectedly, were the services badly disorganised. In a report to the directors in February 1848 Brunel acknowledged that there had been many defects but he refrained from comment other than to say that there was every prospect that they could be overcome and the system then subjected to proper tests. Economical working was impossible at present, he added, because the telegraph was not installed in the engine houses.

Despite all the difficulties however the services were continuing to operate remarkably well. Naturally the problems produced rumours which were greatly exaggerated, particularly by those sections of the press which had been consistently hostile to atmospheric railways. It was partly to counter these rumours and also to help reassure the shareholders that Mr Woollcombe (who later was to become the Company's Chairman) conducted an investigation into the actual running of all the atmospheric service trains between Exeter and Teignmouth during the period from 13th September 1847 to 18th January 1848. This investigation was based on the guard's journals and covered 884 trains over a total distance of 13,481 miles. A double check was made

   (a)   in respect of each journey between Exeter and Teignmouth and back including all stoppages, and

   (b)   in respect of net running times excluding station stoppages for the same journeys.

Regarding (a) the result was:—

Gains and even time

Trains runs to schedule or gained 1 to 5 minutes	513
Trains gained 6 to 10 minutes	252
Trains gained 11 to 15 minutes	25
	790

Losses
Trains which lost 1 to 5 minutes 70
Trains which lost 6 to 10 minutes 14
Trains which lost 11 to 15 minutes 3
Trains which lost over 15 minutes 7
(actual losses were 17, 22, 34, 37, 42, 50 & 56 minutes)

94

In addition to the seven trains which lost over 15 minutes there were three which had to be worked by locomotives so that only a total of ten trains suffered materially due to the atmospheric system.

Regarding (b) the result was even better because 815 trains gained time and against a booked net average speed of 24.77 m.p.h. an average of 28.78 m.p.h. was actually achieved.

During this early period the public clearly had no great cause for complaint. They were probably enjoying a more reliable and certainly a much cleaner service than many locomotive hauled lines could then provide. As time went on however the operating difficulties continued to grow, expenses already much higher than anticipated were still escalating and it became clear that Brunel's optimism could not be justified. In addition to the factors already mentioned:—

(a) the self acting valves in the continuous tube sometimes damaged or destroyed the cup leathers on the travelling piston.

(b) in severe frost the passage of the piston made the leather flap on the continuous tube very liable to crack.

(c) creating the vacuum had an unfortunate side effect in that it tended to draw out the natural oils in the leather so that it was no longer impervious to water.

(d) water accumulated in the tube due to condensation as well as rain.

(e) due to the various defects in the continuous valve breakdowns occurred in the pumping stations. If the valve became unseated to the extent of only 1/1000th of an inch over a half mile of the tube the resulting loss was equivalent to an escape through a 6¼ inch diameter pipe!

(f) the summer weather also provided its seasonal problems. A particularly dry spell in May and June 1848 caused the leather flap to crack and become torn at the joints between the iron plates.

(g) salt in the air caused the iron plates to rust resulting in the rivets working loose — another cause of torn valve leather.

(h) the lime soap caused a hard skin to form on the valve and it proved necessary to substitute a mixture of cod oil and soap as a sealing compound.

(i) insufficient power could be obtained from Maudsley's engines installed at Dawlish.

On top of this formidable list of troubles the volume of traffic was rising and the trains arriving at each end of the atmospheric line tended to become increasingly heavier. This involved working the engines and pumps even harder and it was often becoming necessary to run them at 25 to 30 strokes per minute to create over 20 inches of vacuum instead of at the designed speed of 20 strokes per minute to create 15 to 16 inches of vacuum. This not only strained the motive power even more but was yet another factor to aggravate the damage to the valves; sometimes it was necessary to couple the engines to produce sufficient vacuum to pull the heavier trains and of course operating costs rose even more steeply.

When the accounts for the six months to 30th June 1848 were prepared they disclosed a net loss of £2,487 compared with earlier profits as follows:—

Period 30.5.46 to 31.12.46 .... £5,496
Half-year to 30.6.47 5,105
Half-year to 31.12.47 5,502

Operating costs for the railway as a whole had risen to approximately 110% of the revenue and the atmospheric section was costing 3/1½d. per mile to operate compared with 2/6d per mile on the locomotive hauled sections which, of course, included the heavy gradients. Clearly something had to be done, and quickly.

Because of the problems which had arisen, particularly the escalating costs, the Board appointed an Atmospheric Committee to review all aspects of the system. It will be recalled that this method of propulsion was adopted as being potentially more economical than locomotives but instead it had become intolerably expensive to operate. The Committee comprised Messrs. Gill and Woollcombe, respectively Chairman and Deputy Chairman of the S.D.R., together with Mr Russell, Chairman of the G.W.R. and Mr Buller, Chairman of the B. & E.R. Such an imposing team demonstrates how deeply concerned the Board had become. At their first meeting in July 1848 they called upon Brunel to submit a full report which he made verbally on 1st August, followed by a written submission on 19th August.

It was clear that by this time Brunel's faith in the economics of the system was flagging. He referred at length to all the difficulties which have already been detailed, adding that he did not doubt that great cost reductions could be made after further trials on the existing section but that he could now see no merit in its extension beyond Newton. On the part being operated no cost reduction could be anticipated without renewing virtually the whole of the valve and also having the iron plates painted or preferably zinced or galvanised and made to overlap a little so that both the chemical and mechanical action of the plates on the leather would be eliminated.

The existing valve was not in good condition and he could see no immediate prospect of making it so because renewal would take a year. Money would also have to be spent on the stationary engines which were clearly under-powered.

In conclusion, Brunel did not consider that the Company would be justified in incurring the expense of renewing the valve or altering the engines to make them fully efficient without suitable guarantees from either the patentees or Samuda personally. He still thought however that the apparatus was suitable for supplementary power on the four South Devon banks and suggested that as the engines and tube were nearly ready at Dainton they should be tried if Samuda would maintain the valve.

Samuda, for his part, offered to improve and maintain the valve for a period of twelve months. Pearson considered that, with the introduction of the telegraph into the engine houses, he could get costs reduced very substantially and mentioned a figure of no more than 1/3½d (6½p) per mile given the promised improvements. This contrasted with Brunel's view that he could not get operating costs below 2/– (10p) per mile in under twelve months.

Having obtained these reports the Atmospheric Committee met the full South Devon Railway Company's Board on 28th and 29th August. Gill proposed that Samuda's offer be accepted but he could not get a seconder. The Board then decided that no additional expense by the Company was justified either on valve renewal or improvement to the engines and that notice be served on Samuda to put the valve into thorough repair in accordance with his contract. They also resolved that unless the patentees and Samuda satisfied the directors that the Company would be relieved of its operating losses, then all atmospheric working would cease on 9th September.

Needless to say the shareholders meeting on 31st August was a stormy one. It was held at the Royal Hotel, Plymouth, where only four years earlier the decision to adopt the atmospheric principle was greeted with such enthusiasm. The mood was now dramatically changed and few people had anything favourable to say about the principle or the officers of the Company for adopting it!

Mr Millman suggested that Brunel had led the Company into ruin and complained because in the previous year no explanation had been forthcoming on the grounds that it would damage their own interests. Now he noted that £47,532.11s.8d had been spent on engineering expenses and could only conclude that the engineer had made a good thing out of it. Mr Dunn complained that the Board's detailed investigation should have been made before and not after so much money had been spent and condemned them for relying solely on Brunel despite Stephenson having denounced the atmospheric principle as "a delusive humbug". Mr Ellis commented — "I attend here with some of my brother directors from the Midland Railway and we are all exceedingly disgusted with the atmospheric bauble". Another shareholder, Mr Seccombe, thought it reckless in Brunel ever to have given the least sanction to such a delusive, such an extravagant and such a deceptive system. Others spoke in similar vein and Samuda was attacked as being "as wild a visionary as ever existed".

Two important facts became public knowledge as a result of these discussions. The first was that the Atmospheric Committee's report had not been unanimous since Mr Gill strongly opposed the abandonment of the system. Secondly, the Chairman revealed that the Company was under contract to pay Brunel £6,000 for the construction of the whole line plus an allowance for his staff. When Brunel presented his account it was for a reduced amount for his staff and, as to his own services "in the present difficult position of the Company he could not reconcile it to his mind to take anything". Brunel had in fact worked for the Company for two years for nothing and was still doing so. After this was disclosed Brunel thanked those who had rallied to his side in the debate and added that he had invested £20,000 of his own money in the Company. So Mr Millman's attack on Brunel rebounded.

What now transpired came as a bombshell to the Atmospheric Staff. As recently as 3rd August about eighty men from the Atmospheric Department had been entertained to a supper at the Newfoundland Inn, Newton, to celebrate the opening of the new atmospheric workshops. James Pearson, the Superintendent of that department, addressed the assembly and expressed confidence in the system which he thought had now got over its chief difficulties. The toast — "Success to the Atmospheric" — was then drunk. In a little over a month, on Wednesday 6th September, all the employees in this department received notice that their services would not be required after Saturday, 9th September. Locomotives did in fact take over completely from 6th September.

Notwithstanding all its defects the system worked well right up to the last day. Some material improvements in working linked with cost reduction came shortly before the end when, belatedly the telegraph had been installed in the engine houses. Only ten days before the shut-down a new section of valve was laid at Dawlish using rubber instead of leather, this being but one of many experiments aimed at improvement.

Travellers had undoubtedly looked on the system favourably. After its demise the "Westen Times" wrote — "The change did not occur without an expression of deep regret on the part of a large number of persons who have been accustomed to the atmospheric traction" —

and to this can be added the fact that delays were certainly not eliminated when locomotives took over. Perhaps a fitting epitaph came from the Rev. Treasurer Hawker, B.A. who wrote in 1885 — "I remember travelling by the atmospheric from Newton to Exeter. The motion was very smooth and pleasant; no screaming whistle but a melodious horn was sounded on nearing the stations reminding one of the coaching days of old; no puffing or labouring up the inclines but a swift silent even progress unhasting, unresting; no coke dust or sulphurous smell from the engine".

The end of atmospheric working was by no means the end of the atmospheric story. It took a long time for the dust to settle and legacies remain to this day in the form of excessively steep gradients and tight curves on the line between Newton Abbot and Plymouth.

Thomas Gill had such strong feelings that he resigned from the chair and published a lengthy pamphlet in favour of its continued use. He was able to muster sufficient support to force the Secretary to convene an Extraordinary General Meeting at Exeter on 6th January, 1849. Here Mr Gill disclosed that he had received an offer from Messrs. Clark & Varley to spend £10,000 of their own money experimenting with their own type of atmospheric tube on the S.D.R. If this proved successful they would enter into a five or seven year contract to complete the system at only £5,000 per mile and take a considerable portion of the price in S.D.R. stock. They had also undertaken that working expenses would not exceed 1/- per mile. Bearing in mind that Samuda's system had cost 3/1½d per mile during the half year to 30th June, 1848 and that the hire of locomotives was costing much more than 1/- per mile it was to be expected that many shareholders would fall for this tempting offer and so it was. The meeting dragged on for about eight hours and when finally a vote was taken the result, by those present was:—

Against abandonment .... 645 shares
For abandonment   .... 567 shares.

But victory for the atmospheric was not to be. A poll was demanded and the weight of proxies held on behalf of the holdings of the Associated Railway Companies carried the day, the vote then being:—

For abandonment   .... 5324 shares
Against abandonment .... 1230 shares.

After this meeting Thomas Gill resigned from the Board. His office as Chairman had been taken over by Thomas Woollcombe who had been Gill's Deputy.

It now remains to consider the immediate aftermath and the longer term effects of "The Atmospheric Caper". The first and most important aspect was the financial one. It was the immense cost and that alone which had proved to be the downfall of the system. Much criticism has been made in the past by some who have not taken the trouble to ascertain the facts. It has indeed been described as Brunel's greatest blunder and sympathy has been expressed for passengers subjected to intolerable delays and constant breakdowns etc. What has already been written discounts the criticism of the public service, but there is not doubt that Brunel's reputation did suffer a serious setback.

The total cost of the atmospheric equipment amounted to £433,991. Some was sold off for scrap and some was adapted for other use. By the end of the first year approximately £60,000 had been raised from sales of equipment etc. No further details of sales were published but the total cash realisations appear to have been slightly over £80,000. One of the pumping engines sold was put to use in a lead mine near Ashburton where it became known as the "Brunel Engine" and gave many years of useful service. Some atmospheric pipes were sold much later to the Dartmouth & Torbay Railway Co. and used in an attempt to drain the marshes at Goodrington which were to cause them a lot of trouble and expense. The atmospheric workshop at Newton was taken over to form the nucleus for the running sheds and workshops and the piston carriages were converted for use as brake vans.

The two most unfortunate practical problems which faced the Company resulted from approximately 40 miles of single track as opposed to the double line throughout as originally proposed, coupled with the fact that it was left with no motive power of its own and could not afford to purchase any. In addition, more finance had to be found to complete the lines into Torquay and Plymouth.

Mr Woollcombe immediately set about the task of fending off the creditors and finding the money to pay off overdue debts and to meet the accruing capital and revenue expenditure. Every effort was made to prune expenses and increase revenue but the directors had a lesson to learn regarding the latter — one which unfortunately some of our contemporaries have still not grasped. It was decided to increase fares and at the same time to reduce the service. This the public refused to stomach and traffic was affected to such an extent that the fares were soon brought back to their former level. Thereafter receipts took a turn for the better.

CHAPTER 4

CONSTRUCTION, NEWTON TO PLYMOUTH

Although the line from Newton to Plymouth was completed and opened in three separate stages many of the works were proceeding concurrently; in fact quite a lot had been done even before the first section between Exeter and Teignmouth had been finished.

By the inclusion of steep gradients up to a maximum of 1 in 37 and by following as far as possible the contours of the hills the civil engineering works were kept to a minimum. On the first section to be completed which comprised the 8¾ miles from Newton to Totnes the only important works were a tunnel 272 yards long at the Dainton Summit and a timber bridge to carry the railway over the River Dart immediately before Totnes Station was reached. This station was situated a little over half a mile from the town centre and was modelled on similar lines to the one built at Bridgewater on the Bristol and Exeter line.

This part of the line was single-track throughout with bridge rails. Construction proceeded quite quickly up to the beginning of 1847 but then exceptionally severe weather hindered progress for many weeks. By the middle of March, however, operations were once more in full swing and the line was ready for opening by locomotive-hauled trains on 20th July. It is important to emphasise locomotive working because at this time it was still the intention to continue the atmospheric installations right through to Plymouth. Before the abandonment the engine houses at Dainton and Totnes were completed and the stationary engines built by Boulton and Watt were erected at Dainton, whilst the atmospheric pipes were laid over virtually the whole distance to Totnes.

A party of dignitaries which included H. Champerdowne, the High Sheriff of Devon and J. Derry, the local Mayor, greeted the first train which was due to arrive at 9 a.m. It drew in hauled by the Gooch 2-4-0 locomotive "Pisces" and a seven-foot single "Pegasus" within a minute or so of the appointed time to the accompaniment of cheers from the sightseers and a band playing "See the Conquering Hero Comes!" The sightseers were not alone in their rejoicing at the day's proceedings. Gooch stated that, in his experience, he had never seen Brunel so anxious about anything as he was about this opening. Relying upon atmospheric working Brunel had made the steep inclines and he feared that there would be great difficulty in working them with locomotives. These fears seemed unfounded, however, as all the trains went through very well and it was a great relief to Brunel at the end of the day to find that this was so. He shook hands with Gooch and thanked him for his share in the day's work. As a tribute Gooch added that Brunel never forgot those who helped him during any difficulty.

Doubtless it was intended to complete and open the line to traffic right through from Totnes to Plymouth as a single operation. The reasons why this could not be done are explained later. It is sufficient now to say that the next stage brought the railway only as far as Laira Green which was well outside the boundary of Plymouth and approximately 2¾ miles from the intended terminus at Millbay.

Before reaching Brent there were only two major civil engineering works, these being a viaduct and a tunnel. The viaduct at Rattery comprised six arches each spanning twenty-five feet which were constructed on stone piers. Then, roughly five miles from Totnes came the entrance to the single-bore Marley Tunnel. This was almost half a mile long — 869 yards to be precise — and from a purely engineering point of view it was unnecessary since the territory could have been traversed by a deep cutting. Lord Carew refused to have the railway running over his Marley Estate so, simply to appease him, it had to be taken underground instead.

At Brent came the first of the Dartmoor streams which had to be crossed. This was the River Avon. It was possible to take the railway across this river by a bridge of four arches, but the five to follow were not so easily overcome. These were the Glaze and Lud Brooks followed by the Rivers Erme, Yealm and Piall, in that order. All these had to be spanned by viaducts which were of timber construction on stone piers which rose nearly to the level of the track. Thus they differed materially from Brunel's famous timber viaducts built for the Cornwall Railway. The principal dimensions of these viaducts were:—

Viaduct	Length	Maximum Height
Glaze (Glaze Brook)	163 yards	80 feet
Bittaford (Lud Brook)	117 yards	61 feet
Ivybridge (R. Erme)	252 yards	114 feet
Blachford (R. Yealm)	293 yards	107 feet
Slade (R. Piall)	273 yards	100 feet

The River Plym was easily bridged at Marsh Mills and an embankment then carried the line to its temporary terminus at Laira Green. Immediately beyond that point the Plymouth & Dartmoor Railway had to be crossed, but more about that later.

Completion of all these works was spread over a considerable period but by the end of August 1847 Brunel was able to report that the bridges and viaducts were almost complete, only the parapets and minor accessories remaining unfinished. Between five and six thousand yards of earthworks remained uncompleted and the laying of

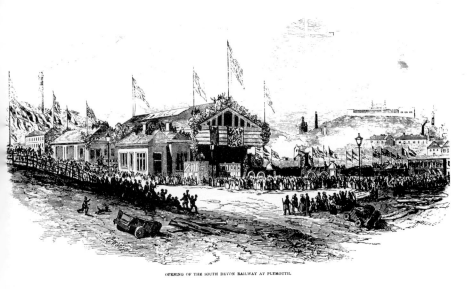

OPENING OF THE SOUTH DEVON RAILWAY AT PLYMOUTH.

The opening of the S.D.R. at Plymouth (Millbay) in 1849 (Courtesy BR Western Region)

An impression by the author of an atmospheric train on the SDR approaching Teignmouth from Newton

"Stag", a member of the "Leopard" class: it was introduced in December 1872. (Real Photos Ltd)

The "Buffalo" class to which "Vulcan" belonged was the last type of goods locomotive introduced by the S.D.R. These were built as "convertibles" but were never converted. "Vulcan" entered service in March 1874. (David & Charles Ltd.)

"Owl" survived as a narrow gauge engine until April 1913 having entered service in January 1873. (David & Charles Ltd.)

A front view of the 0-4-0 Tank "Owl". The width of the broad gauge track is emphasised here. (David & Charles Ltd.)

The S.D.R. owned several 0-4-0 Tank Engines used for shunting. "Raven" was built in November 1874 and spent most of its working life on the S.D.R. in Millbay Docks. Afterwards it was converted to narrow gauge and finished its activities on the Wantage Tramway where it survived until 1919. (Real Photos Ltd.)

"Tiny" was built in 1868 to work the Sutton Harbour branch and replaced haulage by horses. It was referred to as a "coffee pot" engine and was photographed on Newton Abbot Station. It is now in the museum at Buckfastleigh Station. (Author)

Exterior view of Millbay Station probably taken circa 1925. (Mrs J. Matthews)

The first narrow gauge train leaving Millbay Station, 1892. (David & Charles Ltd.)

Plymouth North Road in 1876 (Courtesy Plymouth City Library)

Brent Station in G.W.R. days. The branch to Kingsbridge opened in 1893 started from the bay shown on the left. (David & Charles Ltd.)

The layout at Totnes showing the Brunel type sheds over the platform roads and the atmospheric engine house. (David & Charles Ltd.)

Exeter St. Thomas Station showing overall roof. (David & Charles Ltd.)

East Teignmouth Tunnel about 1880 (Courtesy Bernard & Mills)

A drawing by the author of Ivybridge Viaduct.

ballast was well in hand. At that date none of the permanent way had been laid and the construction of the temporary station at Laira had not been started.

In making this announcement Brunel added that he expected the line to be ready for locomotive working by the end of the year. The Chairman followed this up by reminding shareholders that in 1844 Brunel had forecast that in three years the line would be opened to Plymouth and it was gratifying to learn that this would be fulfilled. Unfortunately though, as with so many of Brunel's optimistic forecasts, it did not come true, because the old enemy, the weather, was to take its toll again.

The track was the same as used on the earlier sections comprising bridge rails on longitudinal timbers. A double line was laid on the Rattery Bank and over the last section from the top of Hemerdon Bank to Laira Green. For the remainder there was only a single line of rails. By February 1848 the weather was still holding up completion of track-laying and Laira Station was still unfinished although everything else had been done. Another two months elapsed however before the line was ready for opening to the public.

The only intermediate station was originally called Wrangaton, but later it was renamed Kingsbridge Road, following a petition from the inhabitants of that town. Additional stations were opened at Brent, Ivybridge and Plympton shortly afterwards but it was not until 1852 that one was provided for the inhabitants of Cornwood.

The first test train to run from Totnes to Laira comprised seven laden trucks, a large wagon and a horse box, the gross load being approximately one hundred tons. It ran on Thursday, 27th April, hauled by "Pisces". All went well and the train arrived at Laira Green at about 2 p.m. to be greeted by many hundreds of people. By 4 p.m. the news of its arrival had spread around Plymouth and the number of sightseers had grown to several thousands. The railway staff were co-operative and the public were allowed on to the station to view the train.

The return journey started just before 5 p.m., the locomotive being driven by Mr M.C. Rea, the Chief Mechanical Engineer, who shortly afterwards transferred to the Great Western Railway as manager of Swindon Locomotive Works. Mr Margery, the permanent way superintendent accompanied him on the footplate. Unfortunately this journey was marred by a fatal accident to a railwayman named Kearley in the course of a shunting operation.

Two days later, on Saturday, 29th April, the Railway Inspector, Captain Symons, made his survey, the journey taking approximately three hours, and on the following Friday, 5th May, the line was opened for passenger traffic. An inaugural special was run from Plymouth comprising one first-class, two second and two third-class carriages headed by the locomotives "Pisces" driven by Mr Gooch and "Cancer" driven by Mr Rea. It left Laira at 8 a.m. with directors and friends aboard and arrived at Totnes at 8.42 a.m. The same two engines hauled the first down train which left Totnes at 10.38 a.m. and arrived at Laira at 11.23 a.m. Once more the weather was perfect for the occasion and tens of thousands thronged to Laira Green, making all the access roads impassable. Although the day was declared a general holiday in Plymouth and all shops and businesses were closed there were no civic celebrations, the absence of which gave rise to a lot of criticism in the local press.

Why, it may well be asked, was a temporary terminus made at Laira Green, such a short distance from Plymouth? There was, in fact, more than one reason, the most important being the action of the Johnson Brothers, who were at the time in control of the Plymouth & Dartmoor Railway, a horse-worked mineral line from Princetown to Sutton Pool, which had been in various kinds of trouble since opening in 1835.

Johnson Bros attempted to get satisfactory terms for the sale of that portion of the works between Crabtree and Sutton Pool which the S.D.R. was authorised to acquire by its 1846 Act. This, however, did not prove easy and negotiations were broken off several times. At some point the S.D.R. had to cross the Plymouth & Dartmoor Railway. The S.D. Company peremptorily attempted to lay its track across the P. & D. line at Laira, whereupon Johnson Bros dumped masses of granite blocks at the crossing point, and these remained until a provisional settlement was reached. Then a level crossing of the two lines was made on the Plymouth side of the embankment. It was not until 23rd April 1851 that a final agreement was negotiated whereby the S.D.R. contracted to pay the Johnsons £13,000 for the line from Crabtree to Sutton Pool.

There were, however, other reasons for delay in proceeding with the works in the Plymouth area. The argument over the location of the terminus there, to which reference was made in Chapter 1, continued over a very long period. Strong pressures were being exerted from various quarters and eventually the Company was obliged to change its plans. One of the provisions in its 1846 Act provided for the abandonment of the terminus at Eldad and the line leading to it from the junction with the proposed Millbay branch. In lieu, the course of the line to Millbay was deviated and a new terminus fixed at a point behind the Octagon. A new branch from Millbay to Devonport in the Parish of Stoke Damerel was also authorised.

The last-mentioned was clearly intended as a sop for the inhabitants of Devonport, but in this the South Devon directors clearly misjudged the feeling of local people. They felt well and truly let down at being served only by a small branch line when they had been promised the terminus of the main line, so they decided to petition Parliament in favour of having what they had been promised. Their Town Clerk was Thomas Woollcombe, one of the South Devon Railway directors, and he was able to convince them ultimately that their proposed action would not be in their best interests in the long term. They took the hint and did not proceed with their petition, but they never forgot that the S.D.R. had let them down.

There were other problems concerning the approach to the new Millbay terminus. The Railway Inspector refused to sanction a level crossing at Union Street and this had to be overcome by raising the line on to an embankment and bridging that street. This was, in fact, just as well as it eliminated the proposed 1 in 25 gradient for which some form of assistant power would have been necessary.

Beyond Laira Green a double line was laid which rose steeply through Lipson Vale to Mutley where a tunnel 183 yards long was built. Here the descent to Millbay commenced, bridges being necessary over the Old Saltash Road (Pennycomequick Hill), Stonehouse Lane (King Street) and, of course, Union Street. The line was surveyed on Wednesday, 28th March, by Captain Symons who was accompanied by the resident engineer, Mr Glennie. The survey train was hauled by the locomotive "Hecla" and, after a thorough inspection, Captain Symons was satisfied that the line was perfectly fit for opening to the public.

When the public opening took place on Monday, 2nd April 1849, a public holiday was declared and peals from the church bells heralded the events of the day. The first train on the scene was in fact the Down mail and quite a crowd had assembled to welcome its arrival at six o'clock in the morning. The formal opening to the public, however, was to come later. At 11 a.m., by courtesy of their commandant, Col. McCollum, the band of the Royal Marines arrived at the station where many of the directors, accompanied by Mr Brunel, Mr Glennie, Mr Hemmett, Mr Martley, Mr Margery, Mr Kerr and other company officials had already assembled. The band formed up and played the National Anthem with quite dramatic effect.

A lengthy train headed by two locomotives had been made up and it included two open carriages in which the band was to travel as far as Plympton. As this train left the station at 12 noon the band struck up "Hearts of Oak" and continued to play as the train proceeded, a contemporary writer declaring that the music drowned the noise from the two locomotives.

At Plympton where, by this time, the station had been opened, several carriages were detached including the two carrying the band which entertained the assembled crowd until the arrival of the Down train which was the "official" opening one. This arrived just before one o'clock and was made up to ten carriages by the addition of those taken off the "Up" train. Again, two locomotives were employed, one being taken over and driven by Mr Martley and the other driven by Mr Rea. The whole train was gaily decorated with bunting, evergreens etc. and as it started on the last lap of its journey the band struck up yet again to the accompaniment of enthusiastic cheers from the spectators.

As the train approached Plymouth the crowds of spectators grew. All vantage points were packed and the Union Nursery Grounds were thrown open for the benefit of a "highly respectable company" to enjoy the spectacle. Union Street on either side of the bridge seemed packed to capacity — it appeared that not only had all the inhabitants of the Three Towns turned out but most of the people from the surrounding neighbourhood as well. The scene was one of the greatest possible animation and the now familiar strains of "See the Conquering Hero Comes!" came from the band as the train entered the station.

CHAPTER 5

MAINTENANCE AND IMPROVEMENT

The operating difficulties caused by the lengthy stretches of single line were aggravated as traffic increased and the division of trains became necessary in order to negotiate the steep banks. In addition there was the problem of late running which had a snowball effect on a single line with passing places. At busy times through trains from Bristol and beyond arrived late at Exeter and this sometimes necessitated running a relief train for local traffic — so adding to the congestion and chaos. Occasionally the situation certainly was chaotic. For example, because of heavy holiday traffic at almost every station on 18th July 1850 some up trains were taking six hours for the journey from Plymouth to Exeter whilst one down train took even longer. Clearly something had to be done about bottlenecks but because of the Company's financial state this was easier said than done. However a survey was made which indicated that the greatest immediate benefit could be derived from doubling the line between Newton and Totnes, a distance of 8¾ miles.

In 1852 a small start was made by laying an additional set of rails for a distance of slightly over ¼ mile at Newton. In the following year a contract was awarded to extend this doubling right through to Totnes. This work, which incorporated a new junction at Aller for the Torquay branch, was completed and opened on 29th January 1855 and cost approximately £30,000. Between 1853 and 1856 improved passing facilities were made at Dawlish, Teignmouth and Kingsbridge Road and considerable alterations to the layout of the lines were made at Totnes to provide increased safety in handling traffic. This then completed all the trackwork deemed essential for efficient train working according to the Chairman who said, in August 1856, that it was not intended to double any further section of the line.

It was not long though before expansion of trade forced a change in outlook and in 1859 powers were sought to double three more sections. These were from Exeter at the west end of the Exe Bridge to Dawlish Station, from West Teignmouth (Old Quay) to the Teign Bridge at Newton and from the west end of Slade Viaduct to Hemerdon. The first two sections were tackled piecemeal, the opening dates being:—

Exe Bridge	— Exminster	1862
Exminster	— Starcross	1860
Starcross	— Dawlish	1874 (25th February)
West Teignmouth	— Newton	1865

The intended doubling between Slade Viaduct and Hemerdon was abandoned.

The last trackworks undertaken to relieve the flow of traffic comprised laying a third set of rails between Newton and Aller in 1874, followed by an extensive crossing loop at Brent in 1875, both measures proving to be of considerable benefit to timekeeping. Preliminary steps were taken however to extend doubling the line. Powers were obtained in 1874 to cover the section between Parsons Tunnel and East Teignmouth where it was proposed to substitute a cutting for the existing tunnel.

Other works were of course required to generate new business and to handle the ever increasing loads. These included opening new stations, extending the facilities at others and laying new sidings to serve various industries along the line. The new stations opened at Exminster and Cornwood in 1852 were for the primary purpose of tapping new areas for trade, but other considerations prevailed in the Plymouth area.

It was only natural that in a large conurbation like Plymouth attempts would be made by some inhabitants to have a station situated more conveniently than Millbay. The first to apply pressure were the wealthy residents of Mannamead, but their application was flatly refused on the grounds that nine-tenths of any possible benefit from such a scheme would go to the local landowners and precious little to the Company! Those in the Mutley area were luckier, however, but only at a price. The Company was far from enthusiastic about building a station here, claiming that little or no extra traffic would be generated, but rather the existing business would be split between Mutley and Millbay. However, if those who wanted the new station there would raise the necessary capital (put variously at £3,500 and £4,000) then the Company would build it. When takings averaged £50 per week for a full year the Company would offer its 5% Preference Stock to individual subscribers in amounts equivalent to the cash put up. This proposition was accepted subject to the Company paying interest at 3% per annum on the money raised pending conversion into Preference Stock. The station was built and opened in 1871. The obligation to construct the large new station at North Road was imposed under the terms of a settlement reached with the L.S.W.R. Although completed by the S.D.R. it was never used by that Company, not being opened until 1877. Reference to this station is made in greater detail in the context of the Battle of the Gauges.

Millbay, the most important station on the line, was extensively enlarged over the years. In addition to its role as the Western terminus it also incorporated the Head Office of the Company where the majority of the shareholders' meetings were held. The original station building was of wooden construction with an overall roof covering three platform roads. The main entrance was at the south end beyond the buffer stops. Hydraulic capstans were installed together with small turntables to enable stock to be transferred from one line to another.

In 1854 negotiations were completed with the Cornwall Railway Board which involved extensions to buildings and trackwork so that the station could be used as an exchange point between the two railways. It was agreed that an occupation rent would be calculated equivalent to interest on the whole of the cost to the S.D.R. and charged to each company in proportion to its traffic. Working expenses were to be apportioned similarly but the entire maintenance costs would be met by the S.D.R. The alterations were completed in time for the opening of the Cornwall Railway on 4th May 1859, but in the following month the South Devon & Tavistock line was opened and it was soon evident that further facilities were required.

So in November 1859 notice was given that powers were being sought:—

(1) To purchase land in Bath Street, Union Street and Millbay Road and to make various alterations to the line levels.

(2) To construct a new goods shed west of the line into the docks with a double-line extension for roughly 100 yards crossing Millbay Road on an iron bridge adjacent to the dock line level crossing.

(3) To widen the track bed from the engine house on the north side of King Street and lay an additional set of rails there.

Commenting on these proposals at a special meeting on 6th December the Secretary emphasised that the works would be costly (the Chairman had complained earlier that land in Plymouth was "as dear as saffron"). The station level would have to be raised considerably to eliminate existing inconvenience and delay. He added that the arrival of one goods train had recently blocked the whole station and 15 trucks had to be sent back to Laira, an operation which involved considerable confusion and expense.

These alterations were largely completed by 1863 and seemed adequate for a time, but by the end of the decade public criticism was becoming rife, culminating in an article in the 'Western Morning News' on 25th August 1870 which condemned the station as dirty and inconvenient. A shareholder drew attention to this statement at a company meeting held on the same day and asked why Plymouth could not have a station befitting the town. The answer came from the Chairman who said that he would be quite happy to see one as splendid as St. Pancras provided that the shareholders were prepared to forego their dividends to pay for it!

To counter proposals by the encroaching Devon & Cornwall Railway for independent stations at Plymouth and Devonport, yet more enlargements were envisaged in 1872 so as to accommodate narrow-gauge traffic, but this scheme was abandoned following an agreement in 1873 whereby the Devon & Cornwall Company obtained what it had originally sought — an independent terminus at Friary. However by its Act of 1874 the South Devon Company was able to acquire more property in Millbay Road to expand its freight facilities. Meanwhile, in 1851, a platform (originally at Starcross) was erected outside the main station where incoming passenger trains were stopped for the examination and collection of tickets. Passengers took a very dim view of the delays caused by this procedure when it was introduced.

At the other end of the line St. David's was another shared station which also served as the terminus of the Bristol & Exeter line. The B. & E. Company were the owners, who initially leased accommodation to the South Devon for £1,300 per annum to include all services. This station had separate Up and Down platforms some distance apart and both built on the City side of the track. This was an inconvenient arrangement and in 1862 the B. & E. Company decided to construct an entirely new complex. The South Devon had to demolish their engine shed to make space for this and build a new locomotive shed on another site at their own expense.

Although the new station was not completed until 1864 the rent charged to the S.D.R. was raised to £3,500 as from 1862. A shareholder questioned this increase which came at a time when traffic was being seriously disrupted by the alterations. He got no satisfactory answer however, and the only conclusion was that the S.D.R. were just in no position to argue about this high-handed imposition. The pill was made more difficult to swallow because the Chairman had already conceded that nine-tenths of the local traffic originated from St. Thomas' Station — hardly surprising as it was more conveniently situated for access to the City Centre and the fares were lower!

The original buildings at St. Thomas were only intended to serve temporarily until arrangements could be completed for sharing St. David's Station. From what has already been said, however, St. Thomas Station was clearly there to stay, so when powers were obtained to double the line from Exeter St. David's to Dawlish in 1859 provision was made for its improvement and enlargement. This work was completed in 1862. The stations at Exminster and Starcross were enlarged during 1853/4 and again in 1861/2.

It seems clear that passenger facilities provided by the S.D.R. were often frugal and sometimes exceedingly so. For many years Dawlish suffered the indignity of a station described by one wit as "an awkward shed which Brunel sketched on the back of an envelope intending it to be a temporary contrivance in the early days of the railway". Perhaps it was fortuitous that this building, almost completely constructed of wood, was burnt down by a spark from a passingg goods train on the night of 21st August 1873 and that the Company had just acquired additional land for a new station which was probably completed much earlier than originally planned.

Newton's original station was of a similar design to that at Exeter with both Up and Down sheds situated on the north side of the line. The Torquay branch trains started from a third shed so the inconvenience here can well be imagined. Under a rebuilding scheme commenced in 1859 and finished in 1861 the three sheds were demolished and replaced by a double-sided junction station. The locomotive sheds were substantially enlarged at the same time. In 1868 the goods yard here was considerably enlarged and in 1873 goods handling at Totnes was improved by laying several new sidings.

Mainly during the 1850's extensive trackwork was laid to serve the docks at Teignmouth. Connections were also made to the lime kilns at Stoneycombe in this period and subsequently a siding was laid to the east of Ivybridge Viaduct to serve the Stowford Paper Mill.

Far and away the most expensive length of line to maintain was that which ran along the coast from Langstone Cliff to Dawlish and Teignmouth. This section was under attack on both flanks, the enemy on one side being the sandstone cliffs and on the other the open sea. There was also some serious damage along the Exe estuary but fortunately along the banks of the Teign and Plym little harm was done by the elements. By 1851 apprehension began to mount concerning the stability of the sea wall and powers were obtained for protective works between Dawlish Warren and Teignmouth.

The first serious trouble came from the cliffs however. It happened on 29th December 1852 at the Breeches Rock between Teignmouth and Dawlish and resulted from exceptionally heavy rainfall. This caused a spring to break out from a soft vein at the back of the cliff which then fell blocking the track and destroying a part of the sea wall. Passengers were conveyed by road between these two towns for two days until temporary repairs enabled travellers to tranfer between trains drawn up to either side of the blockage, an inconvenience which lasted another four days. More smaller slips only caused minor interruptions but at the beginning of February 1853 there was another major fall near Dawlish in circumstances similar to those at Breeches Rock. Although no material damage was then done to the works train services again suffered considerable disruption. Although there were two very severe gales during this winter the sea caused only slight damage in the Dawlish Warren area.

During the ensuing summer a considerable sum was spent in an attempt to make the clliffs safe before the onset of another period of wet weather. The work done mainly comprised drainage and easing the steepness of the slopes and appears to have been quite effective. Nevertheless there may have been some misgivings when, on 1st October 1853, there was a slight fall which deposited debris on the line. Fortunately a young lad working nearby was able to warn the driver of an approaching train in time to stop short of the obstruction which was soon removed. It was not until 1868 that any further work of any consequence was necessary to the cliff face and this was of a precautionary nature at potentially vulnerable places between Teignmouth and Dawlish.

During 1855 the Company received a foretaste of what was in store from the ravages of the sea. Several easterly gales were experienced in the first fortnight of February which caused the beach to be washed away near Teignmouth exposing the marl on which the sea wall was built. A succession of heavy seas then scoured away the marl and despite all the precautions taken resulted in about 30 yards of the wall collapsing. Traffic was immediately halted. The last train to pass was the North Mail on 16th February which had already been delayed for two hours because of other damage done by the combination of a high tide and huge waves whipped up by the violent gale. Severe frosts and the continued turbulence of the sea prevented remedial work and further damage was done on each successive high tide. Before the extremities could be made good more than 50 yards of the embankment carrying the track was washed away. When at last the extremities were secured a wooden viaduct was built on piles across the breach. Although this viaduct was not completed until early in March, traffic was resumed after only a short delay by running trains up to each side of the gap. Passengers were obliged to walk the intervening distance.

Repairs and reinforcements were not completed until August 1856. The wall was rebuilt with deep foundations and a strong buttress footing as had been satisfactorily used elsewhere. This type of reinforcement was added at other potentially vulnerable spots as a precautionary measure. Brunel himself came down from London to supervise all these works.

In December 1858 more easterly gales damaged the wall to the west of Langstone Cliff and here too protective works were incorporated in the repair.

Tuesday, 25th October 1859, saw what one Teignmouth resident described as the worst storm in living memory when it reached its peak at about 5 p.m. Damage was done in many places between Powderham and Dawlish and the line was closed for about 40 hours. By Teignmouth tunnel the parapet was destroyed for about ¼ mile and the sea had played havoc with the track and ballast. There was also considerable damage near Langstone Cliff and at Powderham where the Earl of

Devon's protective river wall collapsed and an inundation from the River Exe washed away several hundred yards of track. Repairs were immediately put in hand by gangs of men recruited locally and traffic was partially restored on the following Thursday morning, but through trains did not resume until that evening. Because of the damage done at Teignmouth on this occasion a new method of dovetailing the masonry was introduced to produce stronger resistance to the action of the sea.

No further damage of any consequence occurred until the winter of 1866/7 when 60 yards of coping on the wall near Dawlish was washed away but this was soon repaired without interrupting traffic. The period of comparative calm was not destined to last much longer however, and on 31st January 1869 the sea-wall at Dawlish sustained its worst battering so far. A strong southerly gale had persisted throughout the night and reached hurricane force shortly after the 7.45 a.m. train had left for Exeter. By about 8 o'clock gigantic waves washing over the line caused a small breach in the sea-wall. Not long afterwards the force of the heavy waves dislodged some wooden supports of an inner wall which fell across the line with a tremendous crash. Within minutes a large section of the sea-wall and about 80 yards of track had been removed by the raging sea at a point between 200 and 300 yards to the east of the station.

Mr Margary and Mr Compton, the traffic superintendent, came by a special train from Plymouth and workmen were soon brought to the scene. It was then that disaster struck again as a further section of the inner wall collapsed killing a nineteen-year old youth, Samuel Coombs, and injuring another workman.

The possibility of constructing a pathway for passengers from one side of the breach to the other had to be abandoned, so that they had to be ferried by road between Dawlish and Starcross. Later, however, arrangements were made for halting trains on either side of the breach with cabs etc. providing transport over a distance of ½ mile only. The traffic situation was aggravated by flood water which not only covered the line between the station and the tunnel entrance but also innundated parts of the town.

The first attempt on Monday, 1st February, to build a temporary sea-wall failed because during the following night continuous heavy seas destroyed all that had been done. A change of tactics on the following day accompanied by calmer waters resulted in success however. A deep trench was made to get right down to the rock foundation and successive layers of green faggots and stones were built up to form an embankment having a good resistance to the action of the sea. Brunel was said to have used this method of construction on previous occasions. Workmen were able to continue throughout the night unimpeded by the comparatively calm sea.

On Wednesday, 3rd February, it proved possible to lay a temporary track across this embankment and work then started on the reconstruction of the sea-wall. Through passenger and goods traffic recommenced on 4th February.

This disaster was attributed to the fact that all the sand had been washed away from the base of the sea-wall. It was decided to remove the offending inner wall and to carry the line slightly inland from its original course. In addition to the cost of ferrying passengers past the breach other expensive arrangements had to be made with the associated companies to enable long-distance passengers arriving late at Exeter to reach their destinations. Ironically passenger traffic actually increased during this period because of sightseers.

The last serious damage in the South Devon era also occurred to the east of Dawlish Station in the winter of 1872/3 when the wall was breached several times. On Christmas Day, 1872, 30 to 40 yards of the wall collapsed into the sea, halting all traffic. Temporary repairs were undertaken but on Tuesday, 31st December, further violent storms reopened the breach, the line was undermined and through traffic stopped once more. A few days later a high tide backed by a strong southerly gale opened this breach yet again. On this occasion a considerable length of the permanent way was washed away. On these occasions passengers were again obliged to cross from one train to another on foot and it was stated that the transfer of luggage caused considerable delays. Bad weather continued and on Saturday, 11th January, another 30 to 40 yards of the wall collapsed. This happened where there was a double track however and trains were able to pass. Layers of faggots and stones were again used to give a temporary foundation until the works could be properly repaired.

It was decided to renew the superstructures of the five viaducts between Brent and Hemerdon with wrought iron girders in place of the outworn timbers. The first two, at Glaze and Bittaford, were dealt with in 1862 followed by Blatchford in 1863. This work was completed in 1864 when the expenditure on Slade and Ivybridge brought the total outlay up to more than £20,000. By this time the wooden piles used in the construction of some of the bridges were showing signs of decay and masonry piers were substituted at the bridges over the Teign and Canal at Newton and the Dart at Totnes. In 1865 the bridge carrying new North Road, Plymouth, over the line by Cornwall Junction was rebuilt with stone piers and by 1868 the bridge over the River Plym at Marsh Mills had been given similar treatment.

Two major tasks were undertaken to improve the permanent way and reduce the cost of renewals. The first was the replacement of the original shillet ballast with broken stone and gravel. This was done in order to improve drainage and so minimise damage to the sleepering which needed replacement far too frequently on account of rot. This operation started in 1855, two of the first sections to be completed being Ratterey Bank in 1856 and Marley Tunnel in 1859. In 1862 Mr Margary mentioned that the sections from Exminster to Starcross and also between Teignmouth and Newton had been reballasted in this way. Four years later this work was still continuing.

The second improvement was the substitution of steel rails for iron ones which had only a comparatively short life. Steel rails were introduced experimentally on the Great Western Railway in 1867 and three years later that Company decided to introduce them extensively on their main lines. It is likely that the South Devon Railway deferred a decision on their use pending the outcome of tests made by other lines but by 1874 they, too, had adopted them as standard for use on the main line.

Although the Great Western was left with a legacy of 14 miles, 60 chains of single track when it took over the South Devon main line in 1876, at least both the track and works had been kept in very good order — which was more than could be said about what they had acquired from the Bristol & Exeter Railway. In fact, in 1871 the S.D.R. Chairman had emphasised that so long as he was at the helm nothing would induce him, either for the sake of dividend increase, or for any other purpose, to neglect to keep the line in a thoroughly efficient state. This was evidenced by the fact that expenditure on the permenant way was running as high as 10% of the gross revenue in the early 1870's.

CHAPTER 6

THE RAILWAY AT WORK

From the small beginnings in 1846 when the length of the line comprised a mere 15 miles of single track between Exeter and Teignmouth the network operated by the S.D.R. grew substantially. Not only did it work its own system but also that of several associated companies, some of which were absorbed before the S.D.R. itself became amalgamated with the G.W.R. on 1st February 1876. By that time it operated the main lines between Exeter, Plymouth, Falmouth and Penzance together with several branches giving an aggregate mileage of 232, as follows:—

S.D.R. Company's own lines	*Miles*	*Chains*
Exeter-Plymouth (Millbay)	52	68
Newton-Torre	5	01
Laira-Sutton Harbour (Plymouth)	1	62
Exeter (City Basin Branch)	0	34
	60	05
Associated lines absorbed		
South Devon & Tavistock (Marsh Mills-Tavistock, absorbed 1865)	12	71
Dartmouth & Torbay (Torre-Kingswear, absorbed 1872)	9	53
Moretonhampstead & South Devon (Newton-Moretonhampstead, absorbed 1872)	12	13
Launceston & South Devon (Tavistock-Launceston, absorbed 1873)	18	76
Total S.D.R. network at 1.2.76	113	58
Associated lines which remained independent		
Buckfastleigh & S.D. (Totnes-Ashburton and Totnes Quay Branch)	10	02
Cornwall Railway (Plymouth (Cornwall Junction) to Falmouth and Lostwithiel to Fowey Branch)	70	07
West Cornwall Railway (Truro-Penzance also Hayle Railway and Branches)	36	11
Torbay & Brixham (Churston-Brixham)	2	06
	232	04

The lines laid around Sutton Harbour and Millbay Docks at Plymouth have not been included, these being regarded as in the nature of sidings or goods yards.

Passenger train services on the main line were generally considered to be adequate for first and second class traffic but varying between poor and really bad for third class or "parliamentary" travellers, although the latter was not always the case.

In the early days when the line was only open between Exeter and Teignmouth there were seven trains in each direction on weekdays and three each way on Sundays. By comparison with other lines accommodation for third class passengers was generous and fares were pitched on the low side. These factors doubtless contributed towards generating traffic which was substantially in excess of expectations. Passengers carried were averaging well over 10,000 per week — i.e. more than 100 per train and weekly receipts were totalling approximately £600. The published time-table for this early period included a rather amusing footnote stating that horses, carriages, dogs and fish would be conveyed but no other description of goods at present!

Despite the popularity of travel and no doubt influenced by the attitudes of the Associated Companies the directors decided to restrict the number of trains carrying third class passengers at the same time as the line was opened to Totnes (July 1847). Although this ill-conceived policy lasted throughout the whole South Devon era it was relaxed somewhat as time went on and it was realised that the third class clientele represented the principal growth area for the future. Nevertheless these generally despised travellers continued to suffer considerable inconvenience and indignity, especially if they were journeying beyond the South Devon Company's own lines. Describing it as "a great boon" the 'Plymouth & Devonport Journal' announced on 25th November 1852 that after the end of that month there would be a third class train all the way to London in one day, leaving Plymouth at 6.55 a.m. and arriving at Paddington at 7.50 p.m. In fact, the published time-table for December 1852 showed that this train arrived at Paddington at 5.0 p.m. No corresponding through Down train was put on for third class passengers at that time — the 6.0 a.m. Down from Paddington, which became known in railway circles as the "Plymouth Cheap" — must have been introduced a little later. As time went on third class travellers were permitted to use additional trains but they were subjected to many restrictions as to the stations between which they were allowed to travel on any particular train.

For example, the June 1865 time-table disclosed restrictions on all the Up trains on which third class accommodation was provided, viz:—

Ex-Plymouth	6.45 a.m.	Restricted to S.D.R. Stations, Reading and Paddington only.
	9.20 a.m.	Restricted to B.& E. Stations beyond Tiverton Junc. and G.W. Stations
	1.45 p.m.	Restricted to Stations to Bristol.
	5.20 p.m.	Restricted to certain return ticket holders for Stations to Brent and passengers for Reading and Paddington.

Needless to say speed on the South Devon main line was severely hampered by the steep gradients and sharp curves. The average scheduled time for stopping trains between Plymouth and Exeter was 2 hours 45 minutes, giving an overall speed of only 18.7 m.p.h. including stops. Even the "express" when it ran non-stop from Plymouth to Newton and also passed Starcross only averaged 27.3 m.p.h., whilst the Down express which additionally passed Dawlish averaged 29.4 m.p.h. Despite the fact that when first introduced the London to Plymouth express was an extension beyond Exeter of what at that time was the fastest train in the world, the journey from Paddington to Laira Green (then the terminus) took 6 hours 50 minute so averaging only 35.7 m.p.h. The Up express completed the journey in five minutes less time. Subsequent years saw a gradual deterioration due to more leisurely running on the B.& E. and G.W. lines so that by 1852 the total journey time had lengthened to 7 hours 35 minutes and the overall speed reduced to 32.6 m.p.h.

It was to meet competition from the L.S.W.R. that the associated companies were compelled to improve upon the performance of their so-called West Country expresses. Beginning on 1st February 1860 the L.S.W.R. reduced its fastest timing between Waterloo and Exeter to 4½ hours. Although this produced an average speed of only 38.1 m.p.h. for the 171½ miles the journey time was 25 minutes less than the best which the broad gauge companies could offer. Both the B.& E.R. and the S.D.R. pressed the G.W.R. for the re-introduction of the 4½ hour schedule which had been in force in earlier years but it was not until 1862 that action was taken. In March that year the "Flying Dutchman" was introduced between Paddington and Torquay. This train departed from London at 11.45 a.m. and was timed to complete the journey to Exeter at an average speed of 56 m.p.h. The greatest difficulty was experienced in keeping to time with this train however and in June 1864 the Didcot stop was eliminated and the average speed to Exeter reduced to 51.5 m.p.h.

It was not until September 1864, when this train was re-routed to terminate at Plymouth, that a reasonably fast train thence to London became a reality with a speed averaging 38.0 m.p.h. in the Up direction and 38.5 m.p.h. for the corresponding Down train. Now, for the first time, it was possible to travel from Plymouth to London and back in a day, but this could not be done in the reverse direction. The timings of the three daily express trains were:—

UP	Plymouth	8.30 a.m.	10.45 a.m.	3.20 p.m.
	London	3.00 p.m.	6.10 p.m.	11.00 p.m.
DOWN	London	9.15 a.m.	11.45 a.m.	4.50 p.m.
	Plymouth	4.35 p.m.	6.10 p.m.	11.55 p.m.

There was at last a train operating on the S.D.R. which could boast an average speed of over 40 m.p.h. for a part if not the whole of its journey. The Down "Dutchman" covered the 214½ miles from Paddington to Newton at an average speed of 40.2 m.p.h.

Travellers between London and the South West were destined to suffer a setback however because not long after the "Dutchman" became a Plymouth train Mr G.N. Tyrell was appointed as superintendent of the Great Western line. He was not favourably disposed towards express trains considering that fairly generous timings produced economy in working. In 1865 therefore the "Dutchman's" timing between Paddington and Bristol was increased but fortunately the Bristol & Exeter Railway was able to make a corresponding reduction in its running time from Bristol to Exeter so maintaining the overall journey time as before. In November 1866 however the "Dutchman" was withdrawn, only to be re-introduced 2½ years later at a reduced speed. Eventually, in May 1871, this famous train had an accelerated schedule for the summer season with a journey time of 6¼ hours between London and Plymouth. It was in this same year that the Boards of the South Devon and the Bristol & Exeter Companies decided to abolish express fares notwithstanding the fact that these continued to be charged by the G.W.R. These moves were aimed at halting the continuing loss of traffic by the broad gauge companies brought about by the faster L.S.W.R. timings between Waterloo and Exeter, a loss which could have been materially reduced had it not been for Tyrell's policy which removed the competitive edge and played into the hands of the L.S.W.R.

There was then little change in the express timings up to the time that the S.D.R. was taken over by the G.W,R. The 1875 time-tables showed a five minute reduction in the timing of the fastest Up express to 6 hours 10 minutes, giving an average speed only marginally under 40 m.p.h. Strangely, however, the Down train continued to have a generous 6¼ hours time allowance despite the fact that it ran non-stop from Newton to Plymouth whereas the Up train was booked to stop at Kingsbridge Road and Totnes!

Turning next to the control of traffic, the signalling was of the "disc and crossbar" type. This involved the erection of a disc and a crossbar on to a revolving post. The disc was set at right-angles to the crossbar. When the disc showed face-on to approaching traffic it indicated all clear, whilst the crossbar fixed full face was the danger signal. The front of the disc was painted black with a large white circle on it and the crossbar was faced in red as an indication of danger. The back of both disc and crossbar was white. A unique signal was placed at Cornwall Junction, Plymouth, known as a double fantail. This comprised a small fantail mounted above a larger one upon a revolving post. When the fantails pointed to the left — i.e. away from the line — the green side was exposed to an oncoming train indicating that the line was clear. When the post was revolved through 180° the fantails pointed towards the line and the red side, denoting danger, was displayed. At night, all clear was indicated by a white light whilst a red light was displayed for danger. Normally each station was protected by only one signal in each direction. Although semaphore signals were first introduced on the G.W.R. system as early as 1st April 1865 it does not appear that they were ever used on the South Devon lines prior to amalgamation.

The telegraph was installed and brought into use at all stations from the time that the first section of line was opened between Exeter and Teignmouth. According to the rules no train should be allowed to depart from any station until it had been confirmed by telegraph from the station ahead that the line was clear. Like so many rules, there were exceptions, and in certain circumstances it was permissible for one train to follow another in the same direction after a specified time interval.

Initially the Company owned and operated its own telegraph system and revenue was raised by its use for non-railway purposes such as the transmission of news. In 1851 the undertaking was leased to the Electric Telegraph Company subject to the retention by the S.D.R. of three lines for internal railway messages. By an Act of 1868 the telegraph system was nationalised and it then became the property of the Post Office. Under the provisions of the Act the S.D.R. received compensation totalling £9,250 together with an annual payment for the use of the Company's poles and certain other services. The Company was still permitted to retain its own telegraph system for railway use. The original instruments installed were of the double-needle type but the S.D.R. was one of the first railways to introduce the absolute block system for working trains when, in 1867, some single-needle block instruments were substituted. By 1876 all the lines operated by the S.D.R. were fully equipped with these single-needle instruments.

As early as 1852 a direct telegraphic link between London and Plymouth was established. On 1st November of that year standard time was introduced and from the same date a time-check signal went out from Paddington to all stations at 10 o'clock each morning.

Crossing trains on the single-line sections was always governed by the working time-tables. Any variations as well as provisions for crossing additional or special trains were fixed by specially telegraphed "crossing orders". The train staff and ticket method of control was never introduced.

All locomotives were fitted with two whistles, one with a deep tone and another having a more high-pitched note. The former was used by the driver when he wished the guards to apply their brakes — hence it became generally known as the brake whistle. For all other purposes the second-mentioned whistle was used. This included the request to the guards to release the brakes for which two short blasts were sounded. During 1859 detonators were introduced for the purpose of protecting any train which was disabled on the line. Facing points were usually operated by capstans and controlled by ground signals painted similarly to the discs. Wire locking of some points in such a way that the signal could not indicate line clear unless the points were correctly set was introduced quite early on. The first installation of fully locking points and signals was made at Totnes in 1873 where a locking frame was put in at a cost of £2,000. Only five of these frames were introduced by the S.D.R. and they were put in only after a considerable lapse of time and probably as a result of pressure by the Board of Trade following an accident which occurred at Torquay on 15th April 1868, details of which are given later in this chapter.

In general operating practices conformed to those on the G.W. and B.& E. lines but there were some notable exceptions. One practice condoned in the 1857 Rule Book certainly seemed to contain an element of risk, viz:—

"It sometimes happens that delay to a Down goods train between Plympton and Plymouth renders it necessary to bring a Down passenger train into Plymouth on the Up line. Whenever therefore the engineman of the train which is on the Down line is passed by another Down train on the Up line between Plympton and the bridge over the Saltash Road he must understand that his train must not pass the Saltash Road Bridge under any circumstances until a switchman or porter be sent from the station to inform him that his train can be admitted to the yard. If that train which is on the Up line overtakes the train which is on the Down line at or below the Saltash Road Bridge both trains must stop upon or immediately before arriving at the Union Street Viaduct to receive further orders".

This was by no means the only operational feature which could be regarded as hazardous or even dangerous and which would not be acceptable in modern times. One, mentioned in the context of damage to the sea wall, was that of bringing trains up to each side of a breach and permitting the passengers to convey themselves and their luggage from a train drawn up to one side of the gap to another train standing on the other side, often in adverse weather conditions. Each train was presumably reversed to the nearest crossing point before the engine could be transferred to the front.

There was a common practice of dividing heavy trains to climb the South Devon banks. Trains were split at the foot of the bank whence the first part was taken up and parked in a siding at or near the summit. The engine then returned to pick up the second part. Upon its arrival at the top of the bank a shunting operation was necessary to bring the two portions together before the whole train continued on its journey. In the case of Dainton summit these proceedings often had to be conducted partly inside the tunnel! More than one instance is recorded when, because of a broken coupling, a train became divided and the front portion was subsequently reversed to look for the missing part.

One of the most astonishing journeys reported took place on the night of Thursday and Friday, 18th/19th July 1850. At the conclusion of an exceptionally busy day a special train had to be put on for passengers travelling down from Exeter towards Plymouth for whom accommodation was not available on the scheduled service trains. This special, it was stated, comprised over 40 carriages and conveyed "upwards of 3,000 passengers". Its scheduled departure from St. David's was at 10.45 p.m. but it was not until a few minutes past 11.0 p.m. that it left St. Thomas's. Near Teignmouth a coupling broke resulting in the last ten carriages being dropped. The front portion was on this occasion taken on to Newton where the unfortunate passengers suffered a two hour delay whilst one of the engines went back to find and bring forward the ten missing carriages. How this mammoth train was divided subsequently to negotiate the banks is not stated but it did not arrive at Plymouth until 6.0 a.m. on Friday morning, having averaged no more than 7¼ miles per hour!

It does seem somewhat surprising that by good fortune no accident arose which was directly attributable to any of the seemingly hazardous procedures adopted. The number of serious accidents recorded is low compared with some lines and clearly demonstrates that the South Devon was a very safe line on which to travel. Details of the principal mishaps are contained in the ensuing paragraphs.

What appears to have been the most serious accident took place at Plympton less than three months after the line into Millbay was opened. A goods train of 7 trucks hauled by the 0-6-0 locomotive "GOLIAH" left Plymouth at 7.30 p.m. on Wednesday evening, 27th June 1849. The train passed Plympton at about 30 m.p.h. and had just begun to climb Hemerdon Bank when an explosion occurred which was heard three miles away. The boiler of the engine had blown up but the only human casualty was fireman Evans. Driver Thompson had a remarkable escape being found in a garden several feet away in a very dazed condition.

It was originally supposed that the accident was the result of what was asserted to have been a fairly common practice, that of screwing down the safety valve to get increased power for the climb up the bank. The evidence of a policeman, James Colman, seemed to support this theory. He testified that he saw the train approaching Plympton at about 30 m.p.h. and noticed that driver Thompson "had the safety valve in his hand".

Driver Thompson however said that the safety valve was set at 73 lbs per square inch and that it was blowing on approaching Plympton. When he gave the engine more steam by the station yard he heard a crack and that was all he could remember. Fortunately Gooch's evidence supported the driver's story. He confirmed that the boiler pressure was fixed at a maximum of slightly over 70 lbs, p.s.i. and added that the boiler should have been able to stand up to a pressure of between 300 and 350 lbs per square inch. It appeared that the explosion was the result of a fracture which occurred near the fire-box door.

The next mishap also involved a goods train. On Tuesday, 5th March a train of 11 wagons hauled by "CORSAIR" was running from Mutley Tunnel to Millbay Station when, due to the slippery state of the rails, it could not be brought under control. Although the speed was estimated at no more than 15 m.p.h. the locomotive crashed through a barrier and a stone wall and finished up in the approach yard to the station about 4 feet above track level. Neither driver Tunstall (who jumped on to the platform) nor fireman Bolt, who remained on the engine, was seriously injured. The local press surpassed itself with the following dramatic description:—

"The neighbourhood of the station was crowded during the day to see the fiery uncontrollable monster against whose power stone walls and massive barriers were of no avail".

The damage to the locomotive could not have been so very serious however because on Monday, 3rd June 1850 it was back again in service hauling an excursion train from Plymouth to Exeter.

A derailment which could have had disastrous consequences occurred near the Breeches Rock between Dawlish and Teignmouth on Monday, 2nd April 1853. The engine and two leading coaches of the 7.35 a.m. Down train from Exeter left the rails and although the locomotive fell over on its side the derailed coaches remained upright and no passengers sustained serious injury. It was ascertained that Charles Moncks who was in charge of this section of the permanent way had left an iron rail across the line. Another boiler explosion took place at Totnes on Tuesday 13th March 1860. The 7.15 Down goods train from Exeter had been hauled as far as Newton by the locomotive "Damon". From there the train was taken to Totnes by the 0-6-0 saddle-tank "Tornado" with driver Moses Hall and fireman Richard Rice. All the shunting operations at Totnes had been satisfactorily completed, the engine had taken on water and the train was standing on the goods shed road awaiting the signal to start. Both the enginemen were on the footplate. Suddenly the silence was shattered by a terrific explosion resulting in the train-load of wagons being pushed back about fifty yards. Driver Hall sustained multiple injuries and was instantly killed, but in contrast fireman Rice had a miraculous escape and despite severe shock he was able to take part in the ensuing clearing-up operations.

On Tuesday 29th July 1862 the 9.20 a.m. stopping train from Plymouth ran into trouble at Ivybridge station. A goods train was standing on the Down line waiting for the 9.20 a.m. passenger train from Plymouth to clear the single line stretch from Hemerdon. As this train approached the goods guard switched the points for some unknown reason. This resulted in a head-on collision, but as the passenger train was slowing down to stop neither engine was derailed or seriously damaged. Almost all the passengers were badly shaken though and there was slight telescoping causing damage to the first compartment of the second coach. Four third class passengers were detained because of injury. A relief engine and carriage was sent on the 10.45 a.m. express from Plymouth and the slow train was reformed and proceeded after the express.

The Plymouth to London mail train came to grief near Rattery on Tuesday, 17th March 1863 on the single track section. The engine became derailed resulting in the coupling with the first coach being broken. The engine then left the track in one direction whilst the following carriages came off the line on the opposite side. Fortunately there were no casualties but the line was blocked for a considerable period during which passengers were transferred from one train to another on either side of the derailment.

Plympton was once more a trouble spot in the early hours of Thursday, 13th September 1866. Shortly before 3.0 a.m. the night goods to Plymouth was halted near Hemerdon due to the locomotive "Brutus" having a bearing which had run hot. A relief engine was summoned from Plymouth which hauled the complete train as far as Plympton where a stop was made. "Brutus" was detached and left standing on the Down road after the train had proceeded towards Plymouth. Some time later the night mail train which was not booked to stop at Plympton Station approached at full speed down over Hemerdon Bank hauled by "Falcon", being in charge of driver Northam and fireman Way. On seeing the signal at danger the brakes were applied and the whistle was sounded but the mail could not be stopped before it collided with "Brutus". "Falcon" and the first coach of the mail were derailed and came to rest in a garden to the south of Plympton Station. Fortunately neither the driver nor the fireman who remained on the locomotive, nor any of the passengers suffered serious injury. Upon realising that a collision seemed inevitable the crew of "Brutus" released the brake, set their engine in motion and jumped clear.

Now a fresh hazard loomed as the unmanned locomotive which had not been derailed steamed towards Plymouth. A message was passed down the line by telegraph giving warning of its approach. The goods train had just been switched from the main line and the warning had enabled "Brutus" to be run into a clear station road whilst everybody was kept away from the danger area. The engine ploughed through to the cloakroom where it became firmly embedded but not a solitary soul was injured. So Dame Fortune smiled twice that morning on the South Devon Railway when what could well have been a double tragedy was avoided.

It was not until the following afternoon that the line was cleared at Plympton enabling normal working to be resumed. At Plymouth Station thousands of sightseers flocked to see the damage which was not however as extensive as when "Corsair" hauling a goods train had crashed there in 1850. The first attempt by three engines to dislodge "Brutus" failed and it was not until the following evening at 5.30 p.m. that she was rerailed. The driver of the mail train was fined £5 and his premium of £7 was stopped for twelve months whilst his unfortunate fireman was dismissed. Mr Brice who was in the travelling Post Office and about to release the Plympton mailbags into the pick-up apparatus was badly shaken and later told a Western Daily Mercury reporter that this was the fourth accident in which he had been involved in the short section between Plympton and Rattery!

On 15th April 1868 a collission took place at Torquay Station attributable to the fact that porter Michelmore forgot to turn the facing points before he took off the Down station signals for a goods train to pass through. In his report published in the following September Col. Yolland, the Government Inspector of Railways, had some harsh things to say because this was one type of accident which it was possible to avoid by mechanical means.

Broken coupling rods or pins were rare occurrences on S.D.R. engines. On 2nd August 1871 however there was such an incident. The 11.45 a.m. "Flying Dutchman" Express hauled by the locomotive "Tiger" was on Hackney Embankment approaching Newton Station when a coupling rod snapped and became badly buckled. Fortunately speed had slackened for the stop at Newton and the train was halted without any further material damage being done. The offending rod was removed before the train proceeded to the station where the locomotive "Etna" took over for the remainder of the journey to Plymouth.

The Chairman was able to boast on 27th August 1874 that the Company had never been forced to pay compensation for killing a single man, woman or child on the railway and expressed appreciation to its officers who had so carefully looked after their interests. This record it seems was retained to the end.

On the subject of timekeeping the South Devon Railway came in for considerable criticism from time to time and from what has already been written some factors giving rise to delays are obvious. The blame did not always lie with this Company, however, because their services were disorganised by the late arrival of through trains from other lines. In these circumstances the S.D.R. sometimes put on a special train for the convenience of their local passengers and for this they made a charge to the associated companies. In 1854 an order was made in the House of Commons for a return of the times of arrival of mail trains following many complaints concerning late running. In this, however, the S.D.R. came out surprisingly well. Of the 124 mail trains with which that company was involved no more than 4 had been delivered on time at Exeter. In 81 instances the S.D.R. had regained some of the time lost before arrival at Exeter and in only 6 cases could any loss be attributed to that company. In two of these cases the locomotive had broken down and in another instance a broken spring had caused delay.

The upsurge of traffic during the summer of 1859 following the opening of the Cornwall Railway was stated to have led to unprecedented disorganisation of the working time-tables. Thirty-five trains were then leaving Millbay Station each day and because of the single lines it just needed one morning train to run late and that could disorganise the traffic for much of the day.

As the stretches of single lines between Exeter and Plymouth were reduced however timekeeping generally tended to improve and this was reflected by editorial comment in the Western Morning News on 25th August 1870. Broadly speaking it was conceded that arrangements for handling traffic were then admirable — commendation indeed from a source which had frequently been highly critical and which seldom seemed to miss an opportunity to denigrate the S.D.R. when the trains — particularly the London Expresses — were running late.

One point must, however, be emphasised. Despite all the imperfections of the atmospheric system and the criticisms levelled against it timekeeping was no worse with that method of traction than with locomotives. Even when additional trains had to be accommodated traffic was generally handled quite efficiently as was amply demonstrated on 2nd August 1848. During the early afternoon two special troop trains arrived at Exeter for Plymouth followed immediately by the Down express which was running late. These three trains were dispatched to Newton in quick succession, the first completing the journey in 38 minutes. At Newton three extra trains were formed up and sent back to Exeter all within a space of 36 minutes, followed shortly afterwards by the Up mail.

CHAPTER 7

LOCOS AND ROLLING STOCK

Reference has already been made to the two 2-2-2 locomotives hired from the Great Western Railway when the first section of the line was opened on 30th May 1846. These, originally named "Snake" and "Viper", were built by the Haigh Foundry in 1838 to meet certain specifications laid down by Brunel. Soon after he was engaged as locomotive superintendent Gooch mentioned in his diary that he doubted their ability even to drive themselves because the cylinders were too small. His prophecy was more or less borne out by events. They were a constant source of trouble and during 1839/40 each was rebuilt by having the 3-2 ratio gearing removed and cylinders altered to 13″ x 18″. After these changes they still failed to perform satisfactorily and it was not until they had ceased to work on the S.D.R. that further changes converted them into reasonably efficient machines. Then the cylinders were increased in size to 15″ x 18″ and the driving wheels reduced from 6′4″ to 6′0″ in diameter.

It was again to the Great Western Railway that the Company turned for the supply of locomotives for all sections not being atmospherically operated until 6th September 1848, and for its entire motive power after that date.

Unfortunately that Company did not possess any passenger engines which were really suited to operate over the heavy banks to the west of Newton. The bulk of the passenger train work was undertaken by locomotives of the "Leo" class. These 2-4-0 tender engines were fitted with 15″ x 18″ cylinders and 5′ driving wheels. Some 2-2-2 locomotives of the "Firefly" and "Sun" classes were also allocated to this task. The former, generally known as "7′ singles", had driving wheels of that diameter. Initially they had 15″ x 18″ cylinders but were subsequently fitted with larger ones with the diameter increased to 15¾″. Then, after 1844, all but three had even bigger cylinders of 16″ diameter and 20″ stroke. It was probably locomotives so fitted which were allocated to the South Devon line. The "Sun" class had 6′ diameter drivers; some had cylinders measuring 14″ x 18″ and on others the diameter was increased to 15″. All were later converted to saddle tanks. For goods traffic 0-6-0 "Hercules" class engines were provided. These had driving wheels of 5′ diameter and cylinders measuring 15″ x 18″.

Even the somewhat more powerful "Leo" class engines were being stretched to a point beyond their capacity in attempting to work heavy passenger trains over these banks. Delays and complaints were commonplace and at the half-yearly meeting held on 29th August 1848, Mr

Dunn a shareholder, complained that these engines were both indifferent and inefficient! (Gooch was in fact obliged to rebuild them later as saddle tanks so as to give them additional adhesion.) However the directors responded by saying that they intended to seek some saving by introducing more suitable locomotives and Gooch was therefore approached. In the following year he had designed and built two 4-4-0 saddle tanks named "Corsair" and "Brigand". These engines had 6' driving wheels and 17" x 24" inside cylinders. The inside sandwich frames did not extend forward beyond the coupled wheels because of the design of the bogie, the centre pin of which was fixed to a bracket on the underside of the boiler. The boiler barrel formed the link between the cylinders and the main frame. Whilst this particular arrangement did not turn out to be entirely satisfactory in the long run these engines performed remarkably well when introduced to their heavy duties on the South Devon banks during August and September 1849.

The G.W.R. was asked to supply additional engines of this type which, incidentally, were the first two locomotives built at Swindon works to be fitted with a bogie. Gooch had already designed a tender version of these locomotives which it was claimed would be able to haul, unaided, a trailing load of 89 tons up an incline of 1 in 40. An estimate was prepared to show the cost of constructing fourteen engines of this class but the G.W.R. steadfastly refused to sanction their construction for the S.D.R. This attitude forced the directors of the latter company to look elsewhere to try to find a satisfactory solution to a problem which was gradually becoming more serious as traffic increased and train loads continued to rise.

But before turning to the next stage in the locomotive saga it is worth referring to the available records to see which G.W.R. engines actually worked on the S.D.R lines. The list that can be given is doubtless incomplete because, excluding "Exe" and "Teign" (which were withdrawn in 1848), it contains only sixteen engines. Fifteen engines are known to have been allocated to work the South Devon lines during the summer months of 1850 and 1851. Furthermore, G.W.R. working extended at least up to 10th October 1854 (when "Cancer" was still at work in Devon) so it is virtually certain that other engines worked over South Devon metals even if only on an occasional special or as a temporary replacement. The known locomotives which worked the line were:—

NAME	CLASS	TYPE
EXE	—	2-2-2
TEIGN	—	2-2-2
PEGASUS	FIREFLY	2-2-2
ANTELOPE	SUN	2-2-2

LANCE	SUN	2-2-2
ARIES	LEO	2-4-0
CANCER	LEO	2-4-0
CAPRICORNUS	LEO	2-4-0
DROMEDARY	LEO	2-4-0
HECLA	LEO	2-4-0
LIBRA	LEO	2-4-0
PISCES	LEO	2-4-0
SCORPIO	LEO	2-4-0
STROMBOLI	LEO	2-4-0
TAURUS	LEO	2-4-0
GOLIAH	HERCULES	0-6-0
CORSAIR	CORSAIR	4-4-0 Saddle Tank
BRIGAND	CORSAIR	4-4-0 Saddle Tank

It was from Brunel and Gooch that the directors sought help when the state of impasse was reached with the G.W.R. The exact role played by each of these two men in the negotiations which followed is not entirely clear. It appears, however, that initially Brunel approached Charles Geach of Birmingham who expressed an interest not only in supplying locomotives similar to "Corsair" and "Brigand" but also in working the line under contract. In May 1850 a draft agreement was submitted to the Company to work the line for a period of ten years. For this purpose twelve 4-4-0 saddle tanks would be supplied for passenger work and four 0-6-0 saddle tanks for goods traffic. The terms proposed were:—

Passenger Trains	Up to 6 coaches (65 tons) between Plymouth and Newton	1/3d per train mile
Passenger Trains	Up to 12 coaches (130 tons) between Newton and Exeter	
Goods Trains	Up to 120 tons between Plymouth and Newton	1/6d per train mile
Goods Trains	Up to 290 tons between Newton and Exeter	

A scale of additional charges for heavier loads was set out and a minimum weekly payment of £298 was to be made. The contractors would be entitled to use the Company's locomotive depots and at the end of the contract the S.D.R. could purchase all locomotives and plant at cost less 2½% per annum depreciation. The amount payable by the Company would be deemed to cover:—

(1) Running charges including enginemens' salaries plus repairs and incidental expenses relevant to the locomotive department.
(2) Interest on capital.
(3) Depreciation.
(4) The contractor's profit.

Because these terms were more favourable than those available from the G.W.R. they were accepted by the Board. In mentioning this fact to shareholders in August 1850 the Chairman was at pains to point out that he was not accusing the G.W.R. of profiteering!

The formal contract dated 3rd June 1851 was negotiated by Brunel, Gooch, Charles Geach and Edward Evans but for some reason only the names of the last mentioned two gentlemen were shown. Gooch's younger brother was placed in charge of the ten-year contract which operated as from 1st July 1851. He also took control of the South Devon Locomotive works at Newton.

Four different firms were involved in building the passenger engines. These were Longridge & Co., Fairbairn & Son, Stothert & Slaughter and the Haigh Foundry, the last mentioned being owned by Edward Evans. These engines became known as the "Comet" class and had 5'9" driving wheels whereas those of "Brigand" and "Corsair" were of 6' diameter. The goods engines, which had 4'9" wheels, were built by the Vulcan Foundry. Both classes were allegedly designed by Gooch and built under his supervision. (According to McDermot, Vol. 2 page 231; but the Chairman's remarks at the February 1852 shareholders' meeting cast considerable doubt upon this.)

The first five of the new passenger engines commenced work during October and November 1851 but the last did not arrive until April 1853. It was not until November 1854 that the first goods engine was delivered, the other three following over the next ten months. Thus it is likely that locomotives continued to be hired from the G.W.R. until some time during 1855. Several years were to elapse before any really tangible financial gain materialised. Whatever savings may have resulted from the lower basic mileage rates and the improved capacity of the engines was swallowed up in other ways. One was the growth of overweight trains. It was frequently becoming necessary to double-head or to divide trains and shareholders were told in 1855 that difficulties had arisen, particularly regarding special contingencies and extras. Evidently the contractors were finding these a source of considerable benefit. Further questions elicited the fact that mileage charges were averaging 1/5½d which compared with a figure as low as 10d per mile shown by the published accounts of some other companies.

Nevertheless the contractors were destined to remain in business with a new extended agreement safely tucked under their belts. The Cornwall Railway, which was opened in 1859 between Plymouth and Truro, was leased to a Joint Committee of Management which comprised the Great Western, the Bristol & Exeter and the South Devon Railway Companies, the last-mentioned having agreed to work the line. Also during the same year the Tavistock and South Devon Railway was opened together with the section of the Torbay and Dartmouth line between Torre and Paignton. Both these undertakings were leased to and operated by the S.D.R. These further commitments necessitated the provision of more locomotives. By this time Geach, one of the original contractors, was dead and his interest had been acquired by Thomas Walker of Wednesbury. So, Edward Evans, Thomas Walker and Daniel Gooch now stepped in with an offer of a new contract to work these lines as well as the S.D.R. system with a promise of somewhat reduced terms as a bait.

It was proposed that the S.D.R. should provide facilities at Newton Abbot for servicing and repairs to all the locomotives to be provided and that there should be through working of engines between the Cornwall and South Devon lines. In the event, the only rate concessions made comprised a reduction in the charge for passenger trains not overweight from 1/3d to 1/2d per mile and a slight modification of the method for charging for excess weights on goods trains. It was estimated that these amendments would save the Company approximately £2,000 per annum. Average speed limits (excluding stops) were to be imposed as follows:—

Passenger trains
East of Newton.............................. 35 m.p.h.
West of Newton .... 30 m.p.h.

Goods trains
On South Devon lines .... 20 m.p.h.
On Cornwall railway........................ 15 m.p.h.

Tentative agreement to these proposals must have been reached quite quickly because by the time a new contract was signed covering a period of seven years from 1st July 1859 eight new saddle tanks for passenger work had already been delivered! The South Devon Railway and the Associated Companies (acting on behalf of the Cornwall Railway) were parties to this new contract.

Twelve new passenger and four new goods engines were provided directly as a result of this contract. The passenger engines were 4-4-0 saddle tanks of the "Hawk" class and came into service between April 1859 and August 1860. These were also designed by Gooch, but their builder was Slaughter & Co. They differed from the "Comet" class in that their driving wheels were 5'6" in diameter and the cylinder bore was 16½" in lieu of 17". Four more locomotives of this most useful class were introduced between September 1863 and June 1865, these being built by the Avonside Co. The four goods engines were 0-6-0 saddle tanks and were delivered by Slaughter & Co. between March and September 1860. The first two of these, named "Dido" and "Hero", had 4'6" wheels and 16½" cylinders whilst the other two had 4'9" wheels and 17" cylinders.

Apart from requirements for working the additional lines a continuing increase in goods traffic throughout the whole system made it necessary to order four further 0-6-0 saddle tanks which were fitted with the larger diameter wheels and cylinders. These entered service between October 1862 and December 1864.

Further extensions to the network operated by the S.D.R. took place during this period. In August 1863 the Cornwall Railway was extended beyond Truro to Falmouth. Then, by August 1864 the Dartmouth and Torbay line was opened right through to Kingswear and in July 1865 the Launceston and South Devon Railway started its service between Tavistock and Launceston. By the end of 1865 the total locomotive stud provided by the contractors had increased to 40, being 28 4-4-0 saddle tanks for passenger work and 12 0-6-0 saddle tanks for goods haulage.

Under the new agreement operating costs continued to be high, to the concern of the Board and the shareholders. Eventually the directors decided that detailed mileage records should be kept for a complete month. The result, revealed at the half-yearly meeting on 28th February 1865, was that computed on an "end to end" basis the contract cost was 1/5.3d per train mile. Perhaps more revealing was the fact that in that month alone an extra 7,801 locomotive miles were run in giving banker assistance or because trains were divided to take them up the banks. If total engine mileage was taken into account the rate was reduced to 1/2.8d per mile.

At the same meeting Mr Woollcombe said that the directors had never pretended that the contract was beneficial to the S.D.R. Hiring the locomotives was forced upon the Company until it was in a position to raise the capital to acquire its own stock.

The view had earlier been expressed that the Company should have had no difficulty in raising capital for this purpose before the expiry of the first contract with Geach & Evans. Perhaps the directors had misgivings because, in 1859, the substantial additions were primarily required to work the associated lines. The shareholders might therefore have objected on the grounds that this would, in effect, largely represent more money being sunk in the Cornwall Railway on which they had already suffered a material capital loss. Be that as it may, events were to prove that the S.D.R. could have profited substantially had they owned and supplied locomotives to the Cornwall and other associated railways on the same terms as the contractors!

It was a foregone conclusion that there was not going to be a further contract when the existing one expired. The shareholders would have seen to that anyway. So arrangements were put in hand to raise the capital required to purchase the contractor's stock. This presented no difficulty and so from 1st July 1866 the South Devon Railway was able for the first time to boast a locomotive stud of its own.

The entire locomotive department of the S.D.R. was placed in the hands of John Wright. He had held a similar post in the employment of the contractors, having succeeded William Frederick Gooch in January 1864.

By 30th June 1868 the stock of broad gauge engines had increased to 49, made up as follows:—

Passenger	"Comet" Class 4-4-0 Saddle Tanks	12
	"Hawk" Class 4-4-0 Saddle Tanks	16
	"Pluto" Class 4-4-0 Saddle Tanks	6
		34
Goods	0-6-0 Saddle Tanks acquired from contractors	12
	0-6-0 Saddle Tanks acquired subsequently	2
		14
	0-4-0 Shunter "Tiny"	1

These particulars were furnished by Mr Wright at the time and differ from information given by McDermot who shows three additional 0-6-0 saddle tanks, "Rosa", "Ada" and "Una", as acquired between January and April 1868. These were presumably acquired somewhat later as it is unlikely that the locomotive superintendent would have overlooked any part of his stock!

It will be observed that another new class of 4-4-0 saddle tanks had by this time arrived on the scene. The "Pluto" class, which had 5'8" driving wheels and 17" cylinders, was built by the Avonside Company. The new goods engines, "Remus" and "Romulus", which had 4'9" driving wheels were acquired in November 1866. By far the most interesting of the new acquisitions was however "Tiny". This engine is unique in many ways. It was reputedly built by Sara & Co. of Plymouth. No such firm of engineers or locomotive builders can be traced as having existed in Plymouth at the relevant time. It is practically certain that "Tiny" was in fact built by Sara & Co. of Penrhyn, Cornwall, who did, in 1868, own a foundry and engine works. It was certainly aptly named, being probably the smallest broad gauge locomotive which ever existed. Of greater significance, it has been preserved and can be seen in the museum at Buckfastleigh station. Its design is unusual having a vertical boiler and cylinders whilst its driving wheels were only 3' in diameter. Acquired in January 1868 to work the Sutton Harbour branch when horses were superseded, it later did service as a shunter at Newton Abbot until 1883. Then it was used as a stationary engine to supply power in the workshops there. Despite her somewhat ungainly appearance she must have performed well as otherwise she would hardly have survived to be restored in 1927 and placed on exhibition.

Up to the commencement of 1872 several more miscellaneous acquisitions were made, mostly of second-hand engines. "Rosa", "Ada" and "Una" have already been mentioned. Built for the Llynvi and Ogmore Railway, they were exchanged for narrow gauge locomotives belonging to the West Cornwall Railway. "Rosa" was a 4-4-0 saddle tank with 5'6" driving wheels and 16½" x 24" cylinders. In 1874 however she was converted into an 0-6-0 saddle tank with 4'6" coupled wheels so making her of similar design to her sisters "Ada" and "Rosa". Whilst general data concerning the remainder of the acquisitions is included as an appendix, some supplementary information is given here regarding some individual locomotives. "Taurus" and "Prince", apart from giving service on the Sutton Harbour branch, were also employed for a while on the B.T. & S.D.R. and also the Torbay and Brixham lines. "King" was ordered by the Torbay & Brixham Company but as they were unable to pay for it delivery was taken by the S.D.R. "Redruth" and "Penwith" came from the West Cornwall Railway and both were converted from narrow gauge tender engines to broad gauge saddle tanks at Newton Works. Although actually shedded at Liskeard, "Penwith" could be seen more often at Millbay Station where, during the day, she was usually employed in shunting the passenger stock. She worked an early passenger train up from Liskeard and returned to that town on an evening working. The boiler of "Redruth" did not steam well and her normal duties were restricted to goods shunting at Millbay.

By this time the writing was on the wall so far as the broad gauge was concerned and all subsequent additions were convertibles, although not all were, in fact, converted to work on narrow gauge lines.

The first of the convertibles comprised a batch of ten 0-6-0 goods engines ordered from the Avonside Co. to meet the continuing increase in freight traffic. These had 4'9" wheels and 17" cylinders and were called the "Buffalo" class. Delivery took place between June 1872 and March 1874. Further orders were placed with the Avonside Co. for four more 4-4-0 saddle tanks, being modernised versions of the "Comets". These comprised the "Leopard" class, two entering service in December 1872 and a further two, ordered later, were delivered in February and March 1875. The last two were replacements for existing "Comet" class engines and bore the same names as the ones replaced. "Lance" had been destroyed in an accident on the Cornwall Railway near St. Germans in December 1873 and "Osiris" had been withdrawn in August 1873 to be used as a stationary engine to work the Portreath incline on the old Hayle Railway.

Lastly, eight 0-4-0 shunters were acquired, also from the Avonside Co., between January 1873 and February 1875. The first three, all delivered in 1873, were well tanks and the remainder were saddle

The best-preserved of Brunel's atmospheric engine houses is at Torre. It was never used for the purpose for which it was built. Now it houses a pottery. (Author)

The atmospheric engine house at Starcross is used as a coal store. A Preservation Order has been made following a request by British Rail to demolish it. (Author)

Totnes engine house (The Brunel Society)

Contemporary drawings of Starcross. (The Brunel Society)

What is believed to be the last remaining fragment of S.D.R. broad gauge track on the West Quay at Sutton Harbour, Plymouth. (Author)

Sections of atmospheric tube awaiting disposal. (The Brunel Society)

*Negotiating a breach following a cliff fall between Teignmouth and Dawlish.
(Courtesy J. V. Somerscocks Esq.)*

*The new viaduct at Slade built in 1893 to carry a double track. This photograph is
of particular interest as it was taken before the girders were removed from the
re-built S.D.R. viaduct. (E. H. Hare Esq.)*

Horse-drawn china-clay train on the Lee Moor Tramway crossing the main line at Laira in 1933. (R. W. Kidner)

At Millbay station in 1933; a 0-6-0ST is shunting Ocean Mail vans. (R. W. Kidner)

The tunnel through Parson and Clerk (Hole Head) about 1910. (Kingsway Series)

Trains passing just West of Dawlish about 1912. (Chapman, Dawlish)

Mutley station in 1933; S.R. train working 'wrong line' due to tunnel repairs. (R. W. Kidner)

Down Riviera Express emerging from Parson & Clerk tunnel in 1930; King Class 4-6-0 No. 6014 (M. W. Earley)

Dawlish Warren station about 1914, with a rail-motor hauling two trailers. (R. W. Kidner Collection)

Plymouth North Road, Up end, in 1933; above a 2-6-0 and 2-6-2T prepare to lift a train of mixed L.M.S. and G.W.R. stock up to Newton; below, engines waiting to return to Laira shed. (R. W. Kidner)

tanks. All had 3' diameter wheels, but whilst the three well tanks had inside cylinders, the saddle tanks had theirs fitted outside the frames. These eight engines spent most of their active lift shedded at Plymouth being mainly engaged in handling traffic passing through Millbay Docks.

Some of the locomotives which were converted to the narrow gauge were quite long-lived. This certainly applied to two members of the "Buffalo" class. "Emperor", which became narrow gauge No. 1317 on the G.W.R. and "Achilles", numbered 1324, were sold to a colliery company in Wales in 1905 and were subsequently owned by the South Wales Mineral Railway. Later they returned once more to the G.W.R. fold, this time as Nos. 817 and 818. The former then survived until October 1926 and the latter until May 1932. "Achilles" had had her name-plate removed long before this. Her active life came to an end at Port Talbot. Another S.D.R. engine which did long service was the shunter "Rook". This little locomotive became narrow gauge No. 1330 when first acquired by the G.W.R., was sold, repurchased in 1924 becoming No. 925 and ended her days at Cardiff in May 1929.

Although the three networks were operated as one system centred on Newton until the amalgamation with the G.W.R. there was a modification in the operating agreement in February 1874. As from that date twenty one locomotives were assigned to the Cornwall Railway Management Committee and eleven were similarly assigned to the West Cornwall Committee. Each committee was thereafter to provide what additional motive power was required to work its line. Neither committee made any additions however and there were therefore 85 locomotives taken over by the G.W.R. as from February 1876.

Finally, a few general notes concerning the locomotives. All carried names but were not numbered. This followed the general practice which existed of naming the stage coaches. From the onset, when contractors supplied the motive power, the Company specified the livery to be used on the locomotives. For the first batch it was stated that the boilers and wheels should be green and the frames finished in brown. The lining out was done in black picked out with red. The fronts of the splashers were decorated with brass and the handrails were of wrought iron encased in polished brass tubing. Nameplates were also in brass. A later specification mentioned dark green paint for the boilers and wheels, vermilion buffers and buffer beams and lining out changed to black edged with white. The lining seems to have been restricted to the bunker and cab-sides (when fitted) and to the valance under the footplating. The tanks appear to have remained unlined throughout. Copper caps on chimneys and brass safety valve covers were a feature of some, but not all, of the engines. Generally the boilers were domeless but again there were exceptions such as the 0-6-0 tanks acquired from the G.W.R. in 1872.

To have been a fireman working over the steep South Devon banks in wet weather when the rails were slippery must have been a hectic and hazardous occupation. In addition to feeding the boiler with water and the fire with fuel it would have been necessary to sand the rails. On the bogie engines the sand box was fitted to the top of the boiler where the fireman did generally have the luxury of a wooden seat on which to sit whilst feeding the sand into a funnel from which it flowed through a forked pipe to the front of the driving wheels. On other engines the sand box was fitted on the front of the engine, in some cases on the buffer beam and sometimes over the smoke-box door, so giving the poor fireman an even more precarious perch when trying to ensure that the engine kept its feet.

In the early days before injectors were fitted water had to be fed into the boiler by ram pumps driven off the crankshaft. For carrying out this operation at stations operating limits were set out within which the locomotive was worked to and fro until the required water level was reached in the boiler.

From the onset it was the policy of the Company to acquire its own rolling stock. It did, however, lack facilities for vehicle construction and for heavy repairs and maintenance. Carriages and wagons were ordered from various outside contractors and the Great Western Railway undertook to carry out the heavy repairs and maintenance in its own workshops.

This arrangement worked quite satisfactorily for both parties until 1st May 1849 when the Bristol & Exeter Railway decided to take over the operation of its line which had hitherto been worked by the Great Western. The upshot of this was that the Bristol & Exeter Company made such exorbitant charges for the conveyance of South Devon rolling stock over its metals that the latter decided to equip its own workshop at Newton to do this work. The tools, plant and equipment originally provided to service the atmospheric plant was adapted for this purpose, so helping in a small way to reduce the loss on the atmospheric venture.

There were two particular periods when, due to increasing traffic, the Company suffered from a severe shortage of passenger carriage stock. The problem first became acute in the mid 1850's when considerable duplication of trains became necessary during peak periods. The difficulties were further aggravated by inadequate workshop facilities and lack of covered accommodation. What stock it did have was deteriorating rapidly and the additional expense which this caused was not being fully matched by increased revenue. Some of the further capital raised in 1856 was therefore earmarked with a view to remedying this situation.

The second serious shortage came about ten years later and extended to goods wagons as well as carriages. Consequently rolling stock had to be hired from the associated companies at great expense which made considerable inroads into the operating profit. To help to overcome this deficiency an allocation of approximately £50,000 was agreed at the half-yearly meeting held on 24th August 1865. This finance enabled orders to be placed with the Metropolitan Carriage & Wagon Co. for additional first, second and third class carriages. 75 goods trucks were also ordered, to be followed by 62 more two years later from the Bristol Wagon Co. Payment for the latter was spread over instalments covering ten years.

By the beginning of 1872 the directors realised that a change to the narrow gauge was inevitable and it was therefore decided that all future stock should be capable of conversion to the narrow gauge with the minimum of expense. The bulk order for new passenger vehicles made in the following year to cover the requirements of both the South Devon and the Cornwall Railways was therefore for "convertible" stock.

By 1876 the fleet of vehicles had risen to 203 passenger carriages and 810 wagons. These figures do not appear to include horse boxes and all the miscellaneous types of vans; neither do they include vehicles allocated to the Cornwall and West Cornwall Railways.

The same deep chocolate livery was used as that adopted by the G.W.R. until 1864 and the carriages had a very squarish and box-like appearance. The first class compartments were well fitted and upholstered, there being four seats on each side. Second and third class travellers were not so well treated. Until well after 1st October 1868, when separate smoking compartments should have been provided by law, the third class carriages were open from one end to the other, the only divisions being provided by the hard wooden seatbacks. In an effort to boost revenue advertising matter was displayed on the sides of some of the stock to the annoyance of some shareholders who particularly objected to the disfigurement of second class carriages in this way.

Continuous vacuum brakes were never introduced, the only carriages to be fitted with brakes being those occupied by a guard. Sufficient brake guards and vehicles were provided as was deemed necessary bearing in mind the length of the train and the gradients involved. Under the Regulation of Railways Act of 1868, every passenger train running for more than twenty miles without stopping had to be fitted with a communication system approved by the Board of Trade between the passengers and the staff in charge of the train. Where introduced, this took the form of a crudely worked communication cord which connected a bell in the guard's van to the engine whistle and ran along the edge of the carriage roofs. It was probably only fitted to the carriages earmarked for express trains. Lighting, when provided, took the form of a roof-fitted oil lamp. The only heating comprised foot-warming pans obtainable at the principle stations and for many years this luxury was only available for first class passengers. There were no toilet facilities or corridors on any trains. These few details give some idea of the joys of travelling in that day and age, but it must be borne in mind that even these conditions were vastly superior to those enjoyed by travellers on the roads.

CHAPTER 8

THE GAUGE WAR

The South Devon Railway Company and its associates played a largely defensive role in the battle of the gauges. Their objective was to keep predators off what they regarded as their territory. Generally the London & South Western Railway directors masterminded the strategy on behalf of the narrow gauge, but this was not always apparent at first sight. At times they even denied involvement! Better results may have been achieved by the associated companies had they used some of the unscrupulous methods of their opponents.

The first attack was launched in 1845 when the Cornwall and Devon Central Bill was promoted for a standard gauge line from Exeter to Falmouth via Bodmin. After this Bill had been rejected the L.S.W.R. illegally acquired the short Bodmin to Wadebridge Railway. Hopes that this would facilitate the passage of the Cornwall and Devon Central Bill when it came before Parliament again were dashed however. Because of its enormous cost it failed in 1846 and again in the following year when a branch to Plymouth was added. This threatened encroachment naturally aroused strong opposition from the S.D.R.

The next encounter came in 1852 after Thomas Gill, ex-Chairman of the S.D.R. had defected to the narrow-gauge camp. Gill helped to promote a line from Plymouth to Tavistock in opposition to the broadgauge South Devon & Tavistock Railway. When the narrow-gauge prospectus was issued on 5th November 1852 an extension from Tavistock to Okehampton and Exeter was included. Whilst Gill was busy whipping up support in Tavistock the L.S.W.R. was similarly engaged in Exeter where the populace was still antagonistic towards the S.D.R. On this occasion each side had its Parliamentary Bill rejected so that honours remained even. Two years later, however, two important landowners switched their allegiance and this tipped the scales in favour of the South Devon & Tavistock Railway Company which received its Act on 24th July 1854.

Other moves were afoot during this period however. The Great Western Board was backing a Bill put forward in 1853 for the Devon & Dorset Railway which encroached into narrow gauge territory. The L.S.W.R. pledged that if this was rejected by Parliament it would introduce a Bill in the next Session to extend its own line from Dorchester to Exeter and possibly on to Plymouth. When the Devon & Dorset Bill was thrown out the L.S.W.R. refused to honour this undertaking. There were probably two reasons for this:—
(1) The Plymouth, Tavistock, Okehampton and Exeter project had

failed to materialise.

(2) A more direct approach to Exeter via Salisbury and Yeovil was being considered.

This new approach to Exeter materialised on 19th July 1860 when a new station at Queen Street was opened. By this time the L.S.W.R. had already drawn up plans for connections to the Bristol & Exeter Railway near St. David's and to the S.D.R. station at St. Thomas' — the latter being strenuously resisted. This led to an agreement whereby:—

(1) The L.S.W.R. dropped the idea of a line to St. Thomas.

(2) The L.S.W.R. was allowed access to St. David's Station by a junction at the west end with full facilities for the interchange of traffic at the station.

(3) A mixed gauge was to be laid between the junction at St David's and Cowley Bridge.

Narrow gauge traffic entered St. David's for the first time on 1st February 1862 but by consenting to this arrangement what the S.D.R. really did was to open the door to the long-planned assault on Plymouth by its rivals.

To this end the L.S.W.R. was backing two projects beyond Exeter to the accompaniment of a major campaign of publicity and propaganda. These schemes were:—

(1) The Mid-Devon & Cornwall Railway which would have linked Tavistock and Launceston with Exeter by a junction with the North Devon line at Coleford.

(2) The Devon Central Railway intended to run from Exeter to Moretonhampstead, Chagford, Okehampton and Lydford on the one hand and to Chudleigh and Newton on the other.

Public meetings were held in various towns to muster support and quite a lot of hypocrisy and mud-slinging was in evidence. Many interests were involved apart from those of the two railway groups. There was, for example, considerable inter-town rivalry and also conflicting interests of landowners, some of whom backed the schemes because they regarded railways as ripe for a good picking, whilst others put up strong resistance so as to preserve their amenities. A few examples will best illustrate some of the tactics being employed.

Mr Charles Gurney, the principal speaker at a meeting convened in Okehampton on 4th November 1859 to support the Devon Central Railway, pulled no punches in a scathing attack on the South Devon Railway. Having condemned its service as hopelessly unreliable because of interruptions resulting from damage by the elements to the coastal stretch of line and by reason of the danger and delay arising from the practice of dividing trains to climb the steep banks he delivered his coup-de-grâce, which was attributed to the Duke of

Wellington. This was that in the event of war the S.D.R. would offer great sport for enemy gunboats who could practise their gunnery by shelling trains as they passed along the coast between Starcross and Teignmouth. What a pity that the First Lord of the Admiralty's views on this alleged pronouncement could not have been expressed by those representing the S.D.R.!

The principal advocate for the Mid-Devon & Cornwall line at a meeting in Plymouth on 12th August 1861 was Sir Lawrence Palk of Torquay. Sir Lawrence, in proposing a resolution in support of this railway, said that there was no desire to invade S.D.R. territory but rather to help them to develop their traffic by connections at Tavistock and Newton. These links, he claimed, would be auxiliaries of vast value to the S.D.R., whereby traffic from Cornwall and Mid-Devon could be brought by that railway to the great markets at Plymouth and Torquay. He could not see how anybody could be against the scheme. He did not reckon however with Mr Woollcombe, the S.D.R. Chairman, who in reply said that whilst agreeing with much that the previous speaker had said regarding objectives he could not approve the means proposed for their attainment. The S.D.R. had no desire to shut up country areas by depriving them of railway facilities. Rather they had their own plans which could be carried out at a moderate cost and in anticipation of a reasonable return on capital. The present ambitious scheme did not have a chance on either count. This judgement proved sound because the necessary financial backing for it never materialised.

Narrow gauge persistence was rewarded following the promotion of a Bill for a railway from Colebrooke to Okehampton. Although the L.S.W.R. alleged that this was an independent project its sponsors insisted that they had their support. Albeit, Parliament authorised the line by an Act of 17th July 1862.

At this time an attempt was made to find some means of ending the constant disputes. This culminated in an agreement dated 23rd October 1862 between the G.W.R., the S.D.R and the L.S.W.R. whereby the last mentioned contracted not to promote or assist any new railway in the South Devon Company's territory. This was defined as a line cutting across the map from east to west immediately below Okehampton. If the broad gauge group now felt some sense of security they were soon to be disillusioned. On 21st May 1863 the Okehampton Company agreed to lease its line to the L.S.W.R. and then on 13th July 1863 secured a further Act for an extension to Lydford. Here it could connect with the broad gauge Launceston & South Devon line giving a connection through Tavistock to Plymouth.

Naturally the South Devon directors were upset because the Lydford extension clearly came within their territory as defined in the agreement made in the previous year. When they protested the L.S.W.R. denied any involvement, but the promoters were still publicly claiming support from that quarter. On 9th November 1863 therefore the S.D.R. requested that the denial be put in writing but this was peremptorily refused by Mr Clarke, the L.S.W.R. Secretary.

It was perhaps unfortunate that in several ways the S.D.R. presented a poorish public image even to the extent of arousing criticism from some of its own shareholders. This of course played into the hands of their opponents. For a considerable period through bookings to L.S.W.R. stations were refused. As a direct result of this the L.S.W.R. (who had no such scruples about through tickets) appointed its own agent in Plymouth in 1862.

In February 1864 a shareholder, Mr Dawe, asserted that considerably more traffic could have been obtained had the S.D.R. dealt more fairly and honestly with the South Western since 1860 and he feared that without a change of attitude that company would get a line from Okehampton to Plymouth. He then referred to a consignment of slate from Newton which the S.D.R. had refused to transfer to the L.S.W.R. at Exeter resulting in the goods having to be sent on by sea. However, a resolution "that the business of the South Devon Railway ought to be conducted with due regard to the public convenience and that it would be to the benefit of this company to facilitate traffic with the South Western Company" was defeated by 92 votes to 12. So it seems the shareholders were prepared to endorse a policy of non-co-operation despite its effect on public opinion and the inconvenience being caused to their Company's customers.

The traders and inhabitants of Devonport were still smarting from the fact that the South Devon Company had for so long withheld what they regarded as proper railway facilities. Also the residents of Tavistock were upset because a junction station at Marsh Mills had never been opened so that passengers travelling up the line had the inconvenience of having to go into Millbay Station and back. The L.S.W.R. was not slow in mustering support in these towns, particularly at Tavistock where there was the prospect of cutting about thirty miles off a journey to Exeter and beyond.

This, then, was the background when in 1865 the Okehampton Company (which changed its name to the Devon & Cornwall Railway on 29th June that year) prepared Bills for an extension beyond Lydford to Stoke Damerel, Plymouth with branches to Devonport, Millbay, Friary and Sutton Pool. The inhabitants of Devonport were so enthusiastic that they sent their mayor to London to present a testimonial personally to the Parliamentary Committee. Even the usual loyalty of Plymothians towards the S.D.R. was not in evidence as they sensed that competition for traffic could do nothing but good.

The Parliamentary Committee decided that the narrow gauge lines should be extended to Plymouth but only by mixing the gauge of the existing track beyond Lydford, with full and equal access for narrow gauge traffic into Millbay, including the Great Western Docks, Sutton Pool and the Naval Dockyards and the provision for the Devon & Cornwall Company of all the accommodation and facilities that they might reasonably require. All the required works were to be undertaken by the S.D.R. on terms and conditions to be laid down by the Board of Trade. Additionally the S.D.R. was obliged to lay a separate narrow gauge line in whole or in part in lieu of the existing single line should this be necessary for the efficient and safe handling of traffic. Four associated companies were in fact involved as owners of sections of the railway over which running powers were granted, viz:—

Launceston & South Devon Railway	Lydford to Tavistock
South Devon & Tavistock Railway	Tavistock to Marsh Mills
South Devon Railway	Marsh Mills to Millbay and Sutton Harbour
Cornwall Railway	Cornwall Junction to Naval Dockyards

All these lines were however operated by the S.D.R. who had put up a spirited fight but neither side could claim complete victory. There is no doubt though that the advantage went to the narrow gauge and at last the L.S.W.R. had the opportunity to run its trains into Plymouth within its grasp. On the other hand the S.D.R. no doubt gained some satisfaction from the fact that independent access to Plymouth was refused.

It will have been noted that the invasion of S.D.R. territory had continued in defiance of the agreement of 23rd October 1862. Several attempts at appeasement by the associated companies were brushed aside before negotiations in 1865 resulted in what became known as the "Quadruple Agreement" between the Bristol & Exeter, the Great Western, the South Devon and the London & South Western Companies. This provided, inter alia:—

(1) For full interchange and forwarding facilities, through rates and fares and equal charges between places served by both broad and narrow gauge groups.

(2) That the L.S.W.R. could subscribe to, work, or acquire narrow gauge companies in Devon and Cornwall and have narrow gauge access to Plymouth, Launceston, Truro, Falmouth and Penzance.

When news of this leaked out strong opposition was voiced by those who had been agitating for the arrival of the narrow gauge in the hope that it would introduce competition and reduce charges. On 25th February 1866 the Plymouth Chamber of Commerce held a special meeting to consider a Bill then before Parliament to ratify the agreement. It was unanimously agreed to petition against the Bill on the grounds that it was against the public interest but as it happened there was a last minute dispute between the B. & E.R. and the L.S.W.R. and the Bill was withdrawn.

By its next move the aggressive Devon & Cornwall Company set out to get not only what it had stood to gain from the Quadruple Agreement but also:—

(1) Completion of a triangle between Millbay Junction and Cornwall Junction, Plymouth, with running powers thereon.

(2) A branch from the Cornwall Railway to an independent station at Devonport.

(3) Running powers over several of the associated companies' existing broad gauge lines between Exeter and Falmouth.

This audacious attempt was contained in a Bill deposited in 1866 but it did not get very far being thrown out in the House of Commons on Standing Orders. But despite this set-back they were doing well. The line from Coleford was opened to within 3½ miles of Okehampton on 8th January 1867 and right through to that town on 5th October 1871. Shortly before then, on 23rd August, notice was served on the three companies involved to mix the gauge on their lines from Lydford to Millbay and Sutton Harbour.

The hope of an independent narrow gauge line beyond Lydford had not been abandoned and a propaganda campaign for this continued unabated. Apart from promoting public meetings, institutions and bodies such as the Devonport Trades Association were cunningly inveigled into passing resolutions in furtherance of this cause. What caused the greatest concern and annoyance in the broad gauge camp, however, was the way in which, wherever and whenever possible, traffic was being poached. This led to a letter of protest from the S.D.R. to the L.S.W.R. on 15th February 1870 which concluded with an offer to re-negotiate the 1862 agreement. This possibly opened the door for the approach made by Daniel Gooch for fresh talks on a Quadruple Agreement. These commenced in November 1871 and resulted in a ratifying Bill being deposited in 1872, but Parliament was then in no mood to stifle competition so the Bill, having been suspended, was later withdrawn. There were further discussions but they came to nothing.

In the same 1872 Session the Devon & Cornwall Company put forward a Bill (which they later amended) which was another attempt to strengthen its position in the Plymouth area. As revised, powers were sought to construct:—

(1) An independent line from Marsh Mills to Devenport via Laira, Friary Gardens and a route roughly parallel to Regent Street,

Coburg Street and North Road.
(2) A branch from this line to Stonehouse Pool.

Despite pressure by the L.S.W.R. to drop this Bill because it might prejudice the renewed attempts then being made to conclude a modified Quadruple Agreement the D. & C. Company refused to do so. The Bill then got as far as the House of Lords before it was rejected, mainly due to opposition by the S.D.R.

To avoid yet another expensive Parliamentary battle an agreement was subsequently thrashed out whereby:—

(1) The D. & C. would construct a 74 chain single line branch from a junction with the Sutton Harbour line to Friary Gardens.

(2) The D. & C. would construct a double-line branch to Devenport, 56 chains long, and a 29 chain branch to Stonehouse Pool. These lines would be narrow gauge only.

(3) The S.D.R. would mix the gauge on the loop between Millbay Junction and Cornwall Junction.

(4) The S.D.R. would provide narrow-gauge sidings at Laira and mix the gauge of the Sutton Harbour Branch as far as Friary Junction.

(5) The Cornwall Railway would mix the gauge on such part of its line as would give narrow gauge access to Keyham Dockyard.

(6) The D. & C. would surrender all rights of access to Millbay Station and Docks and to the Sutton Harbour Branch beyond Friary Junction.

(7) The provisions in the 1865 Act for laying narrow-gauge lines into Millbay Station and Docks and into Sutton Harbour would be repealed.

(8) The S.D.R. would build a mixed-gauge station at North Road which would be under its control but the D. & C. would be entitled to equal facilities for its traffic. Pending completion of this station the D. & C. should have a temporary one for its use.

The temporary station to which reference was made was presumably Mutley. An Act was passed on 7th July 1873 which ratified the agreement.

At about the same time the L.S.W.R. was planning to take over the D. & C. Railway. When terms were agreed between these two companies a Bill was drafted which included powers for the former to acquire and work any lines to be authorised in Plymouth, Stonehouse and Devonport. It was decided later to delete the clauses relating to these lines so as to avoid the risk of antagonising the associated companies. The takeover was sanctioned by an Act of 30th July 1874.

The narrow gauge group scored another partial success during that year. Under the South Devon Railway Act of 1874 the associated companies acquired the Millbay Docks undertaking. Parliament insisted upon the insertion of a clause whereby narrow gauge rails had to be laid from North Road and Cornwall Junctions into and around the Docks. No running powers over these lines were granted to foreign companies however. One more triumph came in 1875 when, despite opposition from the S.D.R., the L.S.W.R. gained access to Sutton Harbour by an independent line from Friary.

The extension from Okehampton to Lydford was opened in 1874. That narrow gauge trains were not allowed through to Plymouth by the end of that year can only be attributed to stalling by the associated companies. Commenting on the S.D.R. accounts for the half-year to 31st December 1874 Mr Hubbard, the new Chairman, stated that an additional narrow-gauge rail had already been laid from Lydford through to Plymouth. Yet it was not until 17th May 1876 that the connecting line at Lydford was opened to permit the first through journey to Plymouth. Various excuses were put forward for the delay. On one occasion it was alleged that the narrow gauge companies had not made their requirements clear whilst at some other time it was claimed that they were making grossly unreasonable demands which could not possibly be met. The fact remains that the S.D.R. did avoid the ignominy of having to admit narrow gauge trains on to its line to Plymouth. By May 1876 the Company had been taken over by the G.W.R.!

CHAPTER 9

FINANCIAL STRUGGLES AND AMALGAMATION

The demand for capital for the construction and development of railways throughout a large part of the nineteenth century was enormous. So as to encourage subscribers to the various schemes put forward the estimated cost shown in the prospectus was frequently understated, being often far lower than the amount ultimately needed for completion. Furthermore, extra calls for capital then followed for additions and improvements. These factors were relevant to the South Devon Railway Company, but they had to overcome a further major hurdle. After the abandonment of the Atmospheric system they were unable to meet their commitments and only narrowly missed being declared bankrupt. Nobody is prepare to invest in an insolvent concern and how the Company was rescued from this parlous state of affairs and turned into a reasonably prosperous enterprise able to raise all the capital it needed in the money market makes an interesting and fairly unique story.

The cost of the whole railway undertaking, including locomotives and rolling stock, was estimated to be less than one and a half million pounds. To meet this the Company was authorised to raise £1,100,000 in ordinary stock and when this was fully subscribed, an additional £365,000 on mortgage or, if the original shareholders agreed, in whole or in part by the issue of additional stock.

The construction of branches to Sutton Harbour, Plymouth and to Torquay was approved in 1846 and it was subsequently decided to extend the latter on to Brixham. Further capital was authorised which brought the total to £2,397,000 by the end of 1848. This materially exceeded the issued capital at that time which comprised Ordinary stock taken up in £50 units, £1,000,000; 6% Guaranteed Ordinary stock in £25 units (later referred to as Preference stock) £500,000; temporary loans and debentures, £478,166, totalling £1,978,166.

The unfortunate atmospheric experiment had cost £433,911. This sum of course covered installations upon only a portion of the railway and made nonsense of Brunel's original estimate of £190,000 for the whole line from Exeter to Plymouth. The loss of a substantial part of this outlay was but one of the financial problems with which the new Chairman, Mr Woollcombe, had to grapple when he succeeded Thomas Gill. Incidentally, it was not until many years later — in 1865 to be precise — that the desperate state to which the Company had been reduced was revealed to the shareholders. The Stock Exchange however was not slow to grasp the seriousness of the Company's position and the £50 shares fell to an all-time low of £5, which prompted the Chairman to observe that there had not been a single railway in the country which had been more the sport of the public than the South Devon. At one time its shares had been boosted to a height that only the insanity of the purchasers could justify; that was just as bad as the present absurd depreciation.

There was, of course, good cause for this depreciation. The Company had defaulted on the interest on its 6% Guaranteed Stock, there was a debt of £241,000 in respect of overdue debentures which the holders were refusing to renew, £96,000 was still due to the contractors for the construction of the line which was still incomplete, other debts were becoming due and there was not a copper in the kitty to meet these huge liabilities. That the railway was able to continue was due solely to the effort and resourcefulness of Mr Woollcombe, something which the proprietors later recognised by a gift of shares which fortunately had then appreciated in value!

On the capital as distinct from the revenue side there was little that the Board could do to economise. They did decide to defer indefinitely the extension of the Torquay line to Brixham and also the construction of the proposed branch to Devenport. The future of the Company and therefore of the railway depended upon how the creditors would react to the situation. Their forbearance would be essential.

Foremost amongst the misfortunes that befall those who get into financial trouble is that none of their affairs can remain private and confidential, but all their deeds and especially their misdeeds are exposed for public scrutiny. The S.D.R. was no exception as the debenture holders, having formed a committee in January 1849 to protect their interests, appointed Mr Hutton, the Official Assignee, to investigate the Company's finances. He found that the books were far from clear and intelligible and had to refer repeatedly to the Secretary or to the Chief Accountant to explain items which under any simple, well regulated system should have been self explanatory. Furthermore, he ascertained that whereas the accounts showed the bank balance at 31st December, 1848, to be £31,227 it was in fact only £2,498. The difference represented a security lodged by a Mr Charles Stevens, presumably to cover his unpaid calls on Ordinary shares. Mr Hutton placed little value upon this asset, so that the accounts became highly suspect.

Meanwhile Mr Woollcombe was beginning to demonstrate his skill as a negotiator by getting the Debenture-holders' Committee to agree to take no proceedings which would embarrass the Company in operating the railway. This was accepted by the majority but there were some holders who were still threatening action for recovery of their money. As further debentures became due for repayment the situation deteriorated and on 6th November, 1849 a special meeting of the Company was called. A resolution was passed giving authority to seek to raise £575,000 in 6% Preference Shares and to apply the proceeds to pay off the overdue debentures and loans. This was despite objections from the Debenture-holders' Committee who advocated an alternative whereby existing holders could either extend their overdue stock or switch to the 6% Preference Stock.

The matter was settled by Parliament who refused to authorise the issue, presumably on the grounds that its prospect of success was minimal. This had an unfortunate repercussion since the Company was then obliged to appropriate the whole of its operating surplus to capital account and to apply it towards the reduction of outstanding liabilities. Undeterred by this setback the Chairman succeeded in persuading the majority of holders to renew their debentures at 6%, being a higher rate of interest than before. There remained those who were still refusing to renew and threatening proceedings. Mr Woollcombe therefore took responsibility for raising a considerable sum on his own personal security to pay off these holders. So he resolved what had been a continuing problem of trying to prevent the Sheriff's Officers from taking possession of the line.

Having resolved the question of the overdue debentures the next problem to be tackled was the large sum still due to the contractors. It occurred to Mr Woollcombe that it might be possible to prevent these creditors from taking proceedings against the Company by offering them some form of security in lieu of cash. But he had to devise something which met the needs of the contractors who had their bills to pay and who had difficulty in raising money on their own security. If they were able to get credit in this way it was only on payment of exorbitant interest rates. This was where the financial genius of Mr Woollcombe came into play. He devised a form of security which guaranteed the payment of both interest and capital on a future stated date. Moreover, like any Stock Exchange security it would be marketable. Agreement was then reached with the contractors who accepted a settlement by this means.

So was born what became generally known as "Lloyd's Bonds". Their use became widespread by railway companies which ran out of funds in the course of construction and Mr Lloyd estimated that at one time there were millions of them in circulation. Credit for their introduction must by right be given to Mr Woollcombe.

At the half-yearly meeting held in August, 1850, Charles Stevens tried to get a vote of no confidence in the Board, whom he accused of apathy and incompetence. His attempt to move a resolution to this effect was then thwarted, but he did secure an Extraordinary General Meeting at the New London Inn, Exeter, on 24th September, 1850, when he was able to propose a resolution, which provided setting up a Committee of three S.D.R. proprietors to consider measures to reduce working expenses, to improve traffic and revenue, and to re-establish the credit of the Company. An amendment was however put forward which expressed confidence in the directors. This was carried by 8,918 votes to 1,664 (including proxies) so that Mr Stevens and his fellow travellers suffered a resounding defeat.

There was still another matter to be settled before the Company was financially in the clear — that being the interest accruing on the 6% Guaranteed Stock which had got into arrear after April, 1848. To deal with this another Extraordinary Meeting was convened at the New London Inn, Exeter, on 12th August, 1851. A capital reconstruction later ratified by Act of Parliament, was then agreed whereby the arrears of interest which had accrued were commuted in exchange for:—

(a)   A guaranteed dividend of 10/9d per share until 1857 and
(b)   In addition to the above the same percentage rate of dividend subsequent to 1857 as may be declared on the £50 ordinary shares.

By this time the tide was beginning to turn and the Company was in a position to raise further capital by way of ordinary stock. The creation and issue of shares to the value of £80,500 was agreed and authorised in 1851, followed by an additional £130,120 in 1852. By August, 1852, the whole of this capital had been taken up. It was at this time that the shareholders expressed their appreciaion for the way in which Mr Woollcombe had rescued the Company by giving him shares to the nominal value of £500.

For the future little difficulty was experienced in finding what capital was required in the open market. Some of the major works for which capital was specifically raised included:—

1857	Construction of the Sutton Harbour Branch	£ 37,970
	Permanent way improvements including doubling the line from Newton to Totnes	£ 79,747
	Improvements to Plymouth Station	£ 28,094
1860	Doubling the line from Exeter to Starcross and improvements at Millbay	£ 30,000
1862	Further outlay on doubling and works at Millbay as above, Exeter locomotive shed and strengthening viaducts	£ 38,970
1865	Purchase of locomotives estimated	£100,000
	Purchase of rolling stock estimated	£ 50,000
	Track doubling Teignmouth to Newton and other permanent way works	£100,000
1873	Track doubling Starcross to Dawlish and laying additional rail for narrow gauge traffic from Lydford to Plymouth	£ 34,000

| 1874 | Further expenditure on foregoing items | £ 47,900 |
| | Locomotives and wagons | £ 26,600 |

Apart from the introduction of Lloyd's Bonds, the S.D.R. pioneered two other forms of fund raising. The first, issued in 1858, was a perpetual as distinct from a dated debenture stock. By this means such financial embarrassment as had occurred after the atmospheric experiment could be avoided. The Company had a stroke of good fortune because on replacing the temporary dated stock a substantial reduction in the interest payable was also achieved. Many of the maturing temporary debentures had borne interest at 6% whereas the majority of the new perpetual stock carried a rate of only 4%. The second innovation, not introduced until 1869, was the "life debenture". This took the form of stock issued at a guaranteed rate of interest throughout the lifetime of the holder and became repayable three months after the Company received notice of the holder's death.

By 1871 the financial strength of the Company had grown to such an extent that it was able to start a reserve fund to meet such contingencies as damages which might be incurred in the event of a serious accident. Fortunately it was not found necessary to draw upon this fund.

To the end however the demand for capital for various purposes continued and as late as 1874 the Company was authorised to raise up to a maximum of £233,000 to cover the acquisition of the Great Western Dock Company's undertaking at Millbay and other capital expenditure envisaged at the time.

After some early set-backs in the field of investment the S.D.R. decided to change its approach by encouraging local branches and other associated undertakings without itself making any material contribution towards the capital required. On 23rd February, 1864, Mr Woollcombe made this quite clear when he told shareholders that branches would be encouraged by offering fair operating terms on condition that local residents provided the necessary finances. It will have been observed that this policy was extended to other projects, e.g. the construction of Mutley Station.

When the Company's affairs had become stabilised with Mr Woollcombe at the helm the railway was run with considerable efficiency, some of the results achieved comparing well with those for the principal lines in the country. The primary objectives of any public carrier should be to seek as much business as possible and then to match the capacity provided with the business obtained. Only in this way can maximum profitability arise, so enabling charges to be held down at levels which the customers are prepared to pay. Then a situation is created which will help to generate growth.

To demonstrate how well the management succeeded on the passenger side figures for the twelve years to the end of 1860 disclosed that receipts per passenger train mile remained within the range from 6/4½d to 7/8d. On other lines the gap tended to be much wider, figures for the L.N.W.R. for example falling as low as 4/7½d in 1849 and rising to a maximum of 6/10½d in 1857, a figure well below the South Devon's best. To attain such good results, particularly having regard to the rural nature of much of the territory served, was indeed a very creditable performance.

Another of the earlier policy decisions to be reversed was the attempt made in 1847 to restrict the availability of third class travel. It was realised that the amount of profit which was obtainable from the first class clientele was strictly limited by their numbers. To bolster business therefore attention had to be focussed on the expansion of second and third class traffic and with thisin view the number of trains catering for third class passengers was increased.

Excursion traffic was successfully developed and the S.D.R. undoubtedly offered facilities far superior to those meted out by some Companies. Travel by excursion trains during the 1860's was described as generally involving long and unearthly hours in packed carriages with queer company, continual shunting aside to enable regular trains to pass and, worst of all, the contempt of ordinary travellers. Although there were certainly some occasions when excursionists on the South Devon had unfortunate experiences, by and large they did quite well and enjoyed their outings.

Despite the occasional error of judgement and consequential setback the general picture was one of steady growth in passenger traffic.

The Company's introduction to the business of carrying mails was not a happy one. Relations with the Post Office were marred by a dispute about charges which was not settled until almost the end of 1849. The price was then fixed at £36.4.5d a day and the S.D.R. received a lump sum of £26,000 which covered the whole of the debt due by the Post Office up to 11th December. Ironically, the shareholders got no solace out of this because it came at the time when the whole of the operating surplus had to be applied to capital account so the beneficiary was the contractor.

Further difficulties arose in 1855 when the G.W.R. travelling Post Office was extended to Exeter. The Post Office authorities then insisted that the S.D.R. should run an additional train for the mails which gave a good connection with this service. This involved expensive amendments to the working time-table the cost of which could not be recovered since no material increase in the number of passengers resulted from the change. In 1860 the North Mail was introduced which connected at Bristol with the Midland Railway's T.P.O. to the North of England.

Apart from the fact that the locomotives available were inadequate for the haulage of heavy goods trains over the South Devon banks another important handicap for freight in the early days was the failure to reach any agreement with the Associated Companies for through transit, so that a lot of time was taken up in transferring goods from one wagon to another at Exeter and Bristol. Then of course there was the further delay for goods going beyond Gloucester caused by the break in the gauge. All this added up to gross inefficiency and prompted the Plymouth, Stonehouse and Devonport Herald, normally sympathetic towards the S.D.R. to suggest that the old stage wagons used to provide a better service.

A few of the publicised complaints will give a background picture. In November, 1849, a consignment of fruit took a whole week to reach Gloucester from Plymouth and a package of copper bolts sent from Birmingham to Plymouth was nine days on the railway. But the classic case was reported on 15th December. Two young men who travelled from Liverpool to Plymouth arranged for their heavy luggage to follow by goods train. It took 14 days to complete the journey and one of the poor lads, who had booked a passage to South America, was obliged to set off on the journey with nothing more than the clothes he stood up in!

The many complaints did not go unheeded and early in 1850 arrangements were made with the Associated Companies for the through transit of goods. As arrangements were concluded in May of the same year for more suitable locomotives to be hired this proved to be the turning point and subsequently efforts were made to get more business and to handle it with reasonable efficiency.

The opening of the Sutton Harbour branch and the development of Millbay Docks both brought good rewards and during 1862 and 1863 the Docks alone provided over 90,000 tons of goods for conveyance. Goods handling facilities at Millbay Station also had to be increased several times to cope with an ever expanding volume of trade.

Perishables, mainly fish and vegetables for the London market, represented another area of considerable expansion, particularly after the opening of the Cornwall Railway. To illustrate the immense volume reached the Chairman estimated that over six million fish were sent from Penzance alone in the half year to 30th June, 1867, and by 1870 through perishable specials from Penzance to Paddington became quite regular features.

By no means all this traffic came from Cornwall however. At Millbay the volume was such that a special platform for handling fish was constructed on the east side of the main station and a covered fish depot was built beside the Millbay Road level crossing. Brixham was, of course, another major source for this traffic.

It was not until 1866, when the Company was able to purchase its own locomotive stock, that operating costs were brought down to a really economical level and the figures produced thereafter demonstrated how remarkably efficiently the railway was being run. Locomotive expenses were reduced from 1/6½d to 9¾d per mile whilst total operating costs were reduced from 52.67% of revenue for the last full year under contract working to 45.48% for 1867, being the first full year after the contract was terminated. Railway expenses throughout the whole country were averaging about 50% of revenue and here was a broad gauge line, reputedly more expensive to run than a narrow gauge one, which had to operate under the handicap of severe gradients, yet able to put up a performance as good as, if not better, than that of any other Company.

There was a steep rise in expenses from 1873 onwards due to rises in the cost of coal, iron and labour. Coal, for example, rose from 15/6d to 26/6d per ton and as a safeguard against the continuing rise in the price of fuel the Company seriously considered the purchase of a colliery of its own. Despite the escalation of costs, which went up from 44.46% of revenue in the half year to 30.6.72 to 54.64% in the similar period for 1873, the S.D.R. retained to the end its reputation as one of the cheapest worked lines in the country.

Two unwelcome burdens in the form of taxation fell fairly heavily on the Company. Stage coaches had been subjected to heavy taxation and Parliament lost no time in ensuring that the switch to rail traffic would not result in any loss of revenue. A railway passenger tax was introduced which was originally fixed at ½d per mile for every four passengers carried, but this was changed in 1842 to 5% of the gross receipts from all passengers. This burden cost the Company £88,066 between 1851 and 1873 and well over £100,000 throughout its entire existence.

Locally railways were regarded as fair game by the rating authorities, some of the smallest sometimes putting in enormous claims if they had the good fortune to have a railway which ran through their territory. The S.D.R. was obliged to contest several excessive assessments.

By 1870 the financial standing of the Company was such as to prompt Herepath's Journal to state that "this . . . line . . . is one of the most improving properties in the Kingdom and in a great measure from good management . . . Hardly any line in the Kingdom is worked so economically as the South Devon. Where the South Devon has economised has evidently been in the train service — not running more trains than are needed for the traffic. The financial position of the Company is remarkably sound".

Not all the existing shareholders seemed so happy about their

Company as did Herepath however. On several occasions they had expressed dissatisfaction with the dividends meted out to them and at the half-yearly meeting in Exeter in February, 1869, some had advocated an amalgamation with the G.W.R. on the basis of an issue to S.D.R. holders of 3½% Guaranteed Stock.

It was not however until the threat of competition from the narrow gauge materialised that this was given serious consideration by the Board and the first positive move was probably taken on 14th January, 1874, when the G.W.R. directors travelled to Torquay to confer with Gooch, representing the S.D.R. and some of the local civic dignitaries. Although no positive proposals came from this meeting it seemed clear from events taking place further up the line that the Company's days as an independent concern were now numbered.

Gooch, in his diary, did not conceal the fact that the G.W.R. was pressurised into making a takeover bid for the Bristol & Exeter Railway at an enhanced price. That Company had written to the G.W.R. in October, 1875, stating that they must offer their line either to the G.W.R. or to the Midland Railway. Having seen the Somerset & Dorset line swallowed up by the L.S.W.R. & M.R. it would have been the last straw from the G.W.R. point of view if the Midland gained control of the B. & E. Railway.

Having watched this manoeuvre the S.D.R. directors no doubt took the view that there would probably be no time like the present to secure an amalgamation with the G.W.R. but there is no evidence of any intimidation such as a threat to invite the L.S.W.R. to make a takeover bid!

Negotiations now proceeded apace and terms were agreed with the G.W.R. in time to be considered by S.D.R. shareholders at a special meeting held on 17th December, 1875. There was sizeable opposition from the ordinary shareholders present on the grounds that better terms should be sought. However the resolution to adopt the terms as agreed was passed, details of the voting being:—

Ordinary Shareholders

Those present represented	£36,000 Stock
In favour of resolution	£23,000 Stock
Against resolution	£13,000 Stock
Proxies represented	£47,000 Stock
In favour of resolution	£47,000 Stock

Preference Shareholders
The voting at their separate meeting was unanimous in favour of the resolution.

An agreement was reached whereby the whole of the South Devon

Company's undertaking was to be worked by the G.W.R. for a period of 999 years from 1st February, 1876. In fact this arrangement did not last as long as 18 months because the two railways became merged under an Amalgamation Act dated 22nd July, 1878, which incorporated the following provisions:—

(1) Every holder of S.D.R. Debenture and Rentcharge Stock would receive in lieu a like amount of stock in the amalgamated Company, this new stock carrying the same rate of interest as before.

(2) S.D.R. 4½% Preference Stock would be exchanged for so much G.W.R. 5% Consolidated Guaranteed Stock as would produce the same income as before and S.D.R. 5% Preference Stock would be exchanged for a like amount of G.W.R. 5% Consolidated Guaranteed Stock.

(3) Every £100 of S.D.R. Consolidated Ordinary Stock would be exchanged for £65 G.W.R. Consolidated Ordinary Stock with the proviso that deferred certificates would also be issued entitling the holder to claim a further £5 G.W.R. Consolidated Ordinary Stock per £100 S.D.R. Consolidated Ordinary Stock at any time after 31st January, 1883.

(4) The S.D.R. Company would be dissolved.

(5) The Amalgamated Company should continue to grant the running powers enjoyed by the L.S.W.R. and D. & C.R. over S.D.R. lines and to enter into agreements with these two Companies for the exchange of traffic, division of receipts, etc.

CHAPTER 10

LATER DEVELOPMENTS
PART 1 — *The GWR Era*

The G.W.R. was far from enjoying a period of prosperity when the S.D.R. was absorbed. The shareholders' dividend was cut in 1874 and reductions followed annually until better times came in 1879. Also the recently acquired Bristol and Exeter main line involved the Company in considerable expenditure to raise it to the standard required by the Board of Trade. The poor state of the track had been blamed for two accidents. So, few funds were available for any improvements on the South Devon main line. Torquay was the only place to benefit from a much needed new station. It was most unfortunate that competition from the L.S.W.R. had to be faced at this time and failure to react promptly and vigorously to their challenge resulted in a substantial loss of business. This was particularly so in the Plymouth area where by 1882 the L.S.W.R. had reduced its fastest timing between North Road and Waterloo to 6 hours 8 minutes with accommodation for all three classes of passengers.

The first serious attempt at a come-back came with the introduction of the "Jubilee Express" in 1887. This train took 6½ hours on the journey from Plymouth to Paddington, but it was the first G.W.R. West-Country express to which third class passengers were admitted. It took until 1890 before the traditional bias against these travellers was finally removed and they were allowed on all trains, but there remained three serious handicaps before competition could be met on equal terms —

(1) the delay and inconvenience caused by the single line sections of the South Devon line

(2) the inability of existing motive power to work at reasonable speed between Newton and Plymouth

(3) the circuitous route from Exeter to London which became dubbed "The Great Way Round".

Before the end of the century a more energetic and enlightened management had taken control and they ardently set about the task of rebuilding the reputation of the G.W.R. and of winning back lost traffic. A major publicity campaign was launched to promote the West Country as an "all the year round" holiday region and this culminated in the introduction in 1904 of the "Riviera Express" (later known as the "Cornish Riviera Express") which created a world record by running non-stop between London and Plymouth, a distance of 246 miles.

Meanwhile, impediments to speed and efficiency were receiving attention. All but one of the single-line bottlenecks had been eliminated by the end of 1893, as follows:

Section	*Date*
Rattery — Brent	} 14 May 1893
Cornwood — Hemerdon	
Ivybridge — Blachford	11 June 1893
Wrangaton — Ivybridge	13 August 1893
Brent — Wrangaton	8 October 1893
Blachford — Cornwood	19 November 1893

Completely new viaducts were built at Glaze, Bittaford, Ivybridge, Blachford and Slade but the original structure at Marley was retained and widened. A new single-bore tunnel was made at Marley and it was here that a serious mishap occurred. Whilst the new tunnel was being bored the original collapsed at one point, completely closing the line for five days. It took until 1st October 1905 to double the final length from Dawlish to the west end of Parson's Tunnel. Widening the five tunnels was completed without stopping the train service. A steel frame was made and mounted on wheels and traffic passed through this frame as the work proceeded.

In 1906 the long-awaited direct line from Exeter to London via Westbury was completed, so reducing the overall distance by twenty miles. Adequate motive power for the South Devon banks had by then been provided from Swindon Works so that at the last G.W.R. was in a position to compete on equal terms with the L.S.W.R. How successful they were can be judged by the fact that travelling between Plymouth and London became almost synonymous with going Great Western.

The development of commuter and other local passenger traffic was being encouraged and to this end unmanned stations termed "halts" or "platforms" were opened. There were four of these on the South Devon main line:

Dawlish Warren (10¾ miles from Exeter)	opened 1st July 1905
Bittaford (39 miles from Exeter)	opened 18th November 1907
Laira (50¼ miles from Exeter)	opened 1st June 1904
Lipson Vale (51 miles from Exeter)	opened 1st June 1904

The halt at Dawlish Warren catered primarily for day-trippers to the seaside from Exeter and was so successful that it was replaced by a manned station in 1912. Those at Laira and Lipson Vale were used as feeders to the suburban services operated in the Plymouth area.

More branch lines were opened. Except for the Brent to Kingsbridge line all were originally independently owned but operated by the G.W.R. throughout. All were ultimately absorbed into the G.W.R. system. Details are:

(1) The Teign Valley Railway, 6¼ miles long from Chudleigh Road

(Heathfield) on the Moretonhampstead line to a terminus near Christow and opened in 1882.

(2) The Exeter Railway, 8 miles in length from a junction on the South Devon main line near St. Thomas to the Teign Valley terminus at Christow. When this was opened in 1903 it made an alternative route from Exeter to Newton and was used occasionally by crack expresses such as the "Cornish Riviera" when the main coastal line was blocked or threatened by exceptionally heavy seas.

(3) The Princetown Railway. This formed a branch from the old South Devon and Tavistock line at Yelverton. It was opened in 1883 and was 10½ miles long. Originally the exchange point was Horrabridge as no station existed at Yelverton until 1885.

(4) The Kingsbridge Branch, 12½ miles long, leaving the main line at Brent. The original intention to extend it to Salcombe was abandoned. It was opened through to Kingsbridge in 1893.

(5) The Yealmpton Branch, opened in 1898. This was 6½ miles long, commencing at the L.S.W.R. station at Plymstock. Access to Plymstock was by a new loop from Mount Gould Junction to Cattewater Junction, Plymouth, and thence over existing L.S.W.R. metals.

To cope with the rapidly rising flow of passenger traffic Plymouth (North Road) station was enlarged in 1908 and major reconstructions were undertaken at Exeter (St. Davids) between 1912 and 1914 and at Newton Abbot in the period 1925 to 1927. A new layout at Exminster was completed in 1931. To help to ease congestion with holiday traffic on the busy section between Exeter and Newton a new cut-off line was proposed in 1935, inland from Dawlish and Teignmouth. This project was abondoned following the outbreak of war in 1939.

Goods traffic expanded surprisingly well bearing in mind that there was so little industry in the area. The majority of the merchandise handled came from outside the region — for example — in the "Up" direction, china clay from Cornwall to the Potteries and perishable goods such as fish, flowers, broccoli and strawberries. These also came principally from Cornwall in transit to the markets of London and the Midlands. There were also substantial imports into Millbay Docks for distribution to various centres up-country. In the other direction the principal commodities were coal and manufactured goods from South Wales, the Midlands and the North for distribution within the area and in Cornwall.

To handle the ever-increasing numbers of wagons new marshalling yards were opened at Laira, circa 1895, Hackney (Newton Abbot) in 1911 and Tavistock Junction in 1916. All three yards were extended periodically. Between 1903 and 1943 loop lines were laid at strategic places to facilitate the flow of traffic. Goods trains could be held in, or diverted into, these loops for such purposes as to create a path for a fast train, to await entry into a busy marshalling yard without blocking the main line or to await the arrival of an engine to give assistance to climb one of the steep banks.

To help to counter competition from road hauliers the G.W.R. developed, from about 1925, its own fleet of lorries to operate a co-ordinated collection and delivery service. Then followed the introduction of express goods trains, many of which were officially named in 1929. There was touch of humour surrounding some of the chosen names, viz, the 10.30p.m. from Reading to Laira was called "The Biscuit". It is difficult to understand why the 5.40p.m. from Pontypool Road to Newton Abbot was titled "The Laira" unless it was a deliberate attempt to cause confusion! The 7.20p.m. from Penzance to Plymouth was more aptly named "The Pasty".

Regarding motive power the facilities at the depot at Plymouth (Millbay) became quite inadequate and as there was no space available for extensions a completely new complex was built at Laira and opened in 1906. This incorporated a typical G.W.R. round-house which had 2 exit and 26 stabling roads. In 1932 the capacity was increased by the construction of an additional engine shed with 4 straight roads.

Several S.D.R. locomotives of the "Comet" and "Hawk" Class were withdrawn shortly after the amalgamation. To fill a temporary shortage ten G.W.R. 2-4-0 "Hawthorn Class" tender engines were converted to saddle tanks to work in South Devon. To replace ageing S.D.R. 0-6-0 goods tanks some of the Armstrong 0-6-0 narrow gauge saddle tanks were converted to the broad gauge. It became a frequent practice in the case of through passenger trains from Bristol and beyond to change engines at Newton Abbot instead of at Exeter. Two of the 4-2-2 Iron Duke Class engines were shedded at Newton for a time — these being "Iron Duke" itself and "Warlock". These engines were quite ineffective beyond Newton however. On one occasion "Lightning" piloted a train as far as Plymouth. Returning light engine she stalled on both Hemerdon and Dainton banks and in each case needed assistance to reach the top! To work the "The Cornishman" which ran non-stop between Plymouth and Exeter three Dean 2-4-0 saddle-tanks, Nos. 3502, 3505 and 3508 were converted to tender engines so that sufficient water could be carried for the journey.

After the gauge conversion in 1892 the practices already mentioned for changing locomotives on through trains were continued until the introduction of the "Duke" class 4-4-0 tender engines enabled through running to Plymouth to become normal. It was not long though before the influence of Churchward was felt with the introduciton of the "Camel", "Atbara" and "City" classes of 4-4-0 locomotives. The exploits of "City of Truro" on an Ocean Mail train on 9th July 1904 have been well publicised. What is not so well known, however, is that over the South Devon line there were many equally brilliant runs with other engines of this class. Whereas "City of Truro" took 59 minutes to cover the journey from Millbay Crossing to Exeter St. Davids, a week earlier "City of Gloucester" with an equivalent load had covered the 52.9 miles in 57¾ minutes to produce an average speed of 55 m.p.h. over this most difficult line.

The powerful and efficient range of locomotives built at Swindon enabled the G.W.R. to adopt a policy whereby, in general, the increasing volume of traffic could be met by higher loadings on existing services rather than by running additional trains. Churchward produced 2-cylinder "Saints" and 4-cylinder "Stars", and the subsequent demands for additional power were met by Collett's "Castles" and "Kings". All these classes of 4-6-0 express locomotives were superbly suited to cope with the hard work required from them in South Devon.

The ever-increasing variety of steam locomotives working on the line became a particular feature in contrast with the near monopoly of saddle tanks of S.D.R. days. Most of the standard G.W.R. classes could be seen, many on regular turns of duty. Some, like Churchward's 4-4-0 Counties, were rare visitors but they did run right through to Plymouth. In the early 1920's for example one would occasionally head the 3.55p.m. "North Mail" out of North Road. A pilot was then needed to give assistance on the banks since this was always a very heavy train. This diversity of motive power extended to locomotives of foreign origin as well as those from other British companies. It is not proposed to try to catalogue the lot but rather to mention some of the most interesting ones.

In 1903 Churchward acquired the first French-built de Glehn Compound 4-4-2 locomotive "La France". This and two others subsequently purchased were extensively tested over the South Devon line against the prototype 4-6-0 express engines which he had built at Swindon. Directly from these trials the "Saints" and "Stars" were developed. A unique visitor in October 1904 was one of Robinson's Atlantics, No. 267, from the Great Central line. This engine worked an excursion train throughout the whole 374 mile journey from Manchester to Plymouth so creating what was then a U.K. long-distance record.

Probably the most publicised locomotive exchanges took place in 1925 when L.N.E.R. Gresley Pacific 4474 "Victor Wild" was in competition with G.W.R. 4074 "Caldicot Castle". In the following year a L.M.S.R. Midland Compound No. 1047 worked between Paddington, Bristol and Plymouth but there does not appear to be any published record as to how she fared on the West Country banks.

Amongst the regular workers were ex-R.O.D. 2-8-0 locomotives of

Great Central origin. A hundred of these were purchased by the G.W.R. after the first world war and there is a record that at least one, No. 3049, was shedded at Laira in 1931. The advent of the second world war saw the arrival of L.M.S. Class 8F and American built Austerities, both being 2-8-0 freight engines. Finally, the Southern Railway must not be omitted. By agreetmen some Southern engines were worked over the G.W.R. line betwccn Exeter and Plymouth whilst G.W.R. locomotives were sent to operate on the Southern route via Okehampton. The object was to familiarise some loco-men with both roads in the event of one being blocked at any time. It was principally West Country Pacifics which were sent to work over the Great Western route.

Whilst under Government control during each of the Great Wars the capacity of the line to handle all the additional naval and military traffic was severly taxed. The second war brought further difficulties when many schoolchildren from London were evacuated to the area. A greater problem was posed, though after Plymouth was blitzed when thousands who worked in the City area sought the comparative peace of the countryside at night either by choice or because their homes had been destroyed. The Yealmpton branch which had been closed to passenger traffic in 1930 had its auto-car service re-instated from 1941 until 1947 by which time the commuter traffic conveyed did not merit its retention. In 1943 a large area of the South Hams was completely taken over for military purposes, all civilians being evacuated. The territory was used primarily by the American Forces as a practice ground prior to the invasion of the Continent. This involved the movement of masses of men and materials into the area, much of which came in by rail over the South Devon line and the branch to Kingsbridge. Needless to say, express trains suffered both in numbers and speed during and immediately after the wars and only really essential maintenance was undertaken.

Although overshadowed by the prospect of nationalisation the G.W.R. was not prepared just to sit back and wait for the inevitable. By the summer of 1946 the non-stop run of the "Cornish Riviera Express" between Paddington and Plymouth had been restored together with the through service from Wolverhampton and Birmingham to Plymouth and Penzance. Furthermore, the threat of coal shortage in the winter of 1946/47 induced the Company to convert some steam locomotives to oil-firing and they were successfully used on this line. The G.W.R. remained enterprising to the end.

Part 2 — After Vesting Day

From 1st January 1948 the South Devon line became a part of the Western Region of British Railways or British Rail as it is now known. A sign that change might be in the air came as early as April 1948 when locomotive interchange trials commenced which extended until July. The line between Exeter and Plymouth was incorporated in two test routes involving engines from other regions as follows:

Paddington to Plymouth via Westbury

Midland Region	4-6-2 No.	46236	"City of Bradford"
Midland Region	4-6-2	46162	"Queen's Westminster "Rifleman"
Eastern Region	4-6-2	60033	"Seagull"
Southern Region	4-6-2	35019	"French Line"

Bristol to Plymouth

Midland Region	4-6-0	45253	
Eastern Region	4-6-0	61251	
Southern Region	4-6-2	34006	"Bude"

These tests provided valuable data for the range of B.R. Standard locomotives the first of which appeared in 1951 and which soon added yet more to the variety of steam to be seen in this territory.

1955 saw the introduction of the railway modernisation plan which presaged the untimely demise of steam. Whilst the Western Region opted for diesel-hydraulic power the preference elsewhere was for diesel-electrics. Through working of the latter ensured the continuance of a wide range of motive power in the new era. A feature of the transition was the sight of double-heading over the banks by a mixture of steam and diesel traction. An appropriate celebration to mark the last days of steam was laid on on 9th May 1964, exactly 60 years after the record-breaking run by "City of Truro". Whilst the performance of No. 7029 "Clun Castle" on a special train over the same route did not match that of "City of Truro" it was nevertheless a memorable occasion.

Plymouth (Laira) was chosen as the site of the prototype for W.R. diesel maintenance and servicing depots. This was partially opened in 1960 and completed in the following year. The steam depot at Laira remained open until June 1965 but in the last few years it was used almost entirely for locomotives operating on the old Southern Region line after the Friary Sheds had been closed. A diesel servicing depot also existed at Newton Abbot but this was closed in 1981.

Before road competition had materially dented the fortunes of the line there was one major area of growth. This was the seasonal holiday traffic which did not reach its peak until towards the end of the 1950's.

All the holidaymakers to and from South Devon and Cornwall had to be conveyed over the section between Exeter and Aller, the junction for the Torbay branch. The vast majority chose to travel on summer Saturdays during the school vacation period so resulting in the handling of up to a hundred trains in each direction in one day. Apart from Saturday specials to and from such places as London, Glasgow, Newcastle, Hull, Nottingham, Liverpool and Manchester many scheduled trains ran in two or more parts. Some would be loaded up to fifteen or sixteen coaches whilst a number would convey a large proportion of standing passengers. Add to this the fact that several trains stopped at Teignmouth and/or Dawlish whilst others were supposed to run non-stop the chaos can be well imagined as soon as the inevitable late-runners began to upset the schedules. The proceedings on the Down line degenerated into a crawl, stopping in every section, the procession extending at times well to the east of Exeter. Undertaking the monumental task of handling such vast numbers with its consequential overcrowding, congestion and delay doubtless accelerated the determination of many of the travellers to use their own transport in future!

It soon became evident that the anticipated benefits from the modernisation plan were being offset by the effects of road competition and escalating costs. Under his terms of reference Dr Beeching was left with no alternative but to wield the axe, but the impact of this on the railways in the West Country was traumatic. Main lines as well as branches were closed. The South Devon line is now no more than a trunk cut off at its base (Millbay), denuded of most of its branches but with a few short stumps remaining. All that is left of British Rail's branch network is that portion of the Kingswear line as far as Paignton and the section of the Moretonhampstead line to just beyond Heathfield, the latter open for mineral traffic only. A part of the Ashburton Branch between Totnes and Buckfastleigh and also the remainder of the Torbay line from Paignton to Kingswear still exists however. These are privately owned and used to operate steam trains as a tourist attraction during the spring and summer. Of the nineteen passenger stations and halts which were open at one time west of Exeter (St Davids) only eight remain, these being Exeter (St Thomas), Starcross, Dawlish Warren, Dawlish, Teignmouth, Newton Abbot, Totnes and Plymouth (North Road).

The closure of small stations conformed to a policy directed towards the encouragement of long-distance passengers at the expense of local traffic. In this context credit must be given for the development of "Inter-City" trains which have produced a far superior service between South Devon, the Metropolis, the Midlands and the North than had ever existed before but this has been achieved to some extend by lighter loadings than in the days of steam. The introduction of the "Golden Hind" in 1964 produced, for the first time, a regular scheduled run between Plymouth and Paddington of under 4 hours. The timings were 235 minutes in the up direction and 230 minutes down with three intermediate stops. Before the introduction of this schedule a trial non-stop run was made with a seven coach train in 208 minutes notwithstanding a long permanent way slack. The locomotive involved was 1027 "Western Lancer". In 1968 a 3¾ hour schedule was brought in for the "Cornish Riviera Express" with stops at Exeter and Taunton. In the following year the Taunton stop was omitted and with reversion to a limited load (in this instance 9 coaches) the time was reduced to 3½ hours. Now with the High Speed Train the fastest timing has been cut to 3 hours 4 minutes. In this context further alterations were made at the Laira depot in 1980/81 for the maintenance and servicing of H.S.T's.

Railway management was largely responsible for the run-down in freight haulage. It was decided that the carriage of goods by the wagon-load and the maintenance of small depots to serve local needs was uneconomic. Concentration was the "in" thing. After Cornwood was closed in 1959 there remained thirteen goods stations on the South Devon line until 1963. Savage cuts up to 1967 reduced the number to three, viz, Exeter, Newton Abbot and Plymouth. The Millbay depot was closed in 1966 when all the local goods traffic was transferred to the ex-Southern depot at Friary. Coal traffic for the whole of Devon and Cornwall was brought only as far as Exeter by rail whence it was distributed by road so that its carriage on the South Devon line came to an abrupt end. A "Freightliner" service was introduced for Plymouth but this was soon withdrawn because it did not pay.

The first casualty amongst the marshalling yards was Laira. This was closed in 1959 to make way for the new diesel depot. 1971 saw the closure of the Tavistock Junction and Hackney (Newton Abbot) yards and also the removal of the rail connection to Millbay Docks.

The carriage of china clay from Cornwall, Ivybridge and the Newton Abbot area, cement from Plymstock and oil to the Cattewater, Plymouth, now constitutes the bulk of the revenue-earning merchandise which is carried and the total volume is trivial compared with that handled in the 1950's.

What of the future? Plymouth Station is, fortunately, one of the principal sources of passenger revenue on Western Region. So long as this position is maintained the continued existence of the South Devon line must be assured. There seems scope for yet more improvements in speed and efficiency. The potential of the High Speed Train is severely restricted on account of the numerous sharp curves and multiple aspect of signalling has only been installed from the West of Totnes to

Plymouth. The possible development of a diesel version of the Advanced Passenger Train, installation of multiple aspect signalling throughout and the accompanying track simplification should produce much shorter journey times and so improve the railway's competitive position.

A fitting conclusion to the South Devon saga should include a reference to the great architect of the line and to the age of steam. On 7th October 1954 the record was established for the fastest steam-hauled run from Plymouth to Paddington. The 227½ mile journey by an Ocean Mail Express from Millbay Docks was completed in 3 hours 37 minutes to produce an overall average speed of 62.9 m.p.h. The locomotive, Castle Class No. 5069, could not have been more aptly named. It was Isambard Kingdom Brunel!

APPENDIX 1 — STATION DETAILS

Approx Mileage	Station	Opened to Traffic Passenger	Goods	Closed to Traffic Passenger	Goods	Notes
0	Exeter (St. Davids)	30.5.1846	1.5.1847	Still Open	Still Open	Previously open for B. & E.R. Traffic
1	Exeter (St. Thomas)	30.5.1846	Not Handled	Still Open	—	Temporarily closed 2.4.1917 to 3.3.1919
5	Exminster	1852	*1852*	30.3.1964	4.12.1967	Precise date of opening not known
8½	Starcross	30.5.1846	*1.5.1847*	Still Open	4.12.1967	
10½	Dawlish Warren Station	23.9.1912	*23.9.1912*	Still Open	5.8.1963	Temporarily closed 1.1.1917 to 1.5.1919
10¾	Dawlish Warren Halt	1.7.1905	Not Handled	29.3.1912		—
12	Dawlish	30.5.1846	*1.5.1847*	Still Open	17.5.1965	
15	Teignmouth	30.5.1846	1.5.1847	Still Open	4.12.1967	
20	Newton Abbot	30.12.1846	1.5.1847	Still Open	Still Open	
29	Totnes	20.7.1847	6.12.1847	Still Open	4.12.1967	
36	Brent	5.5.1848	*5.5.1848*	5.10.1964	6.4.1964	
38	Wrangaton	5.5.1848	*5.5.1848*	2.3.1959	9.9.1963	Traffic to M.O. Defence siding still handled
39	Bittaford	18.11.1907	Not Handled	2.3.1959		—
41½	Ivybridge	5.5.1848	*5.5.1848*	2.3.1959	29.11.1965	Traffic to china clay siding still handled
43½	Cornwood	1852	*1852*	2.3.1959	2.3.1959	Precise date of opening not known
48	Plympton	15.6.1848	13.9.1848	2.3.1959	1.6.1964	
50	Laira Green	5.5.1848	*5.5.1848*	2.4.1849	1.5.1849	
50¼	Laira Halt	1.6.1904	Not Handled	7.7.1930		—
51	Lipson Vale halt	1.6.1904	Not Handled	22.3.1942		— G.W.R. trains ceased to call after 7.7.1930 then used by S.R. only
51½	Mutley	1.8.1871	Not Handled	3.7.1939		—
52	North Road	28.3.1877	'' ''	Still Open		
52¾	Millbay	2.4.1849	*1.5.1849*	23.4.1941	20.6.1966	

Dates in Italics — These are assumed dates which it has not been possible to verify.

SCHEDULE of S.D.R. LOCOMOTIVES

Name	Builder	(a) Date Built & (b) Date Acquired by S.D.R. if Different	Class	Type	Dimensions		G.W.R. Broad Gauge No.	Nar Gau No
					Driving Wheels	Cylinders		
(1)	(2)	(3)	(4)	(5)	(6)	(7)	(8)	(9
Comet	Longridge & Co.	Oct 1851	Comet 4-4-0 ST		5'9"	17"x24"	2096	-
Lance	do	do	do	do	do	do	Scrapped 12,	
Rocket	do	do	do	do	do	do		
Meteor	do	Nov 1851	do	do	do	do	2097	
Aurora	do	Jan 1852	do	do	do	do	2098	
Priam	Haigh Foundry	Nov 1851	do	do	do	do	2099	
Damon	do	Feb 1852	do	do	do	do	2101	
Falcon	do	Sep 1852	do	do	do	do	2102	
Orion	do	Feb 1853	do	do	do	do	2103	
Ostrich	Wm. Fairbairn & Son	Aug 1852	do	do	do	do	2104	
Ixion	Stothert & Slaughter	Apr 1853	do	do	do	do	2105	
Osiris	do	do	do	do	do	do	Withdrawn 8/	
Tornado	Vulcan Foundry	Dec 1854	-	0-6-0 ST	4'9"	do	2139	-
Volcano	do	Nov 1854	-	do	do	do	2140	-
Goliah	do	Sep 1855	-	do	do	do	2141	-
Sampson	do	do	-	do	do	do	2142	-
Eagle	Slaughter Gruning & Co.	Apr 1859	Hawk 4-4-0 ST		5'6"	16½"x24"	2106	-
Elk	do	do	do	do	do	do	2107	-
Hawk	do	do	do	do	do	do	2108	-
Lynx	do	do	do	do	do	do	2109	-
Gazelle	do	May 1859	do	do	do	do	2110	-
Mazeppa	do	do	do	do	do	do	2111	-
Giraffe	do	Jun 1859	do	do	do	do	2112	-
Lion	do	do	do	do	do	do	2113	-
Antelope	do	Jul 1859	do	do	do	do	2114	-
Wolf	do	Aug 1859	do	do	do	do	2115	-
Tiger	do	May 1860	do	do	do	do	2116	-
Hector	do	Aug 1860	do	do	do	do	2117	-
Cato	do	Sep 1863	do	do	do	do	2118	-
Dart	do	Dec 1864	do	do	do	do	2119	-
Pollux	do	May 1865	do	do	do	do	2120	-
Castor	do	Jun 1865	do	do	do	do	2121	-
Dido	do	Mar 1860	-	0-6-0 ST	4'6"	do	2143	-
Hero	do	Apr 1860	-	do	do	do	2144	-
Hebe	do	do	-	do	4'9"	17"x24"	2148	-
Ajax	do	Sep 1860	-	do	do	do	2149	-

ame	Builder	(a)Date Built & (b)Date Acquired by S.D.R. if Different	Class	Type	Dimensions Driving Wheels	Cylinders	G.W.R. Broad Gauge No.	G.W.R. Narrow Gauge No.
(1)	(2)	(3)	(4)	(5)	(6)	(7)	(8)	(9)
rutus	Slaughter Gruning & Co.	Oct 1862	-	0-6-0 ST	4'9"	17"x24"	2150	-
rgo	do	Oct 1863	-	do	do	do	2151	-
tlas	do	do	-	do	do	do	2152	-
uno	do	Dec 1864	-	do	do	do	2153	-
orgon	do (now Avonside Engine Co.)	Sep 1866	Pluto	4-4-0 ST	5'8"	do	2122	-
luto	do	Oct 1866	do	do	do	do	2123	-
edley	do	do	do	do	do	do	2124	-
ol	do	Nov 1866	do	do	do	do	2125	-
itan	do	Oct 1866	do	do	do	do	2126	-
ebra	do	do	do	do	do	do	2127	-
emus	do	Nov 1866	-	0-6-0 ST	4'9"	do	2154	-
omulus	do	do	-	do	do	do	2155	-
iny	Sara & Co.	Jan 1868	-	0-4-0 WT	3'0"	9"x12"	2180	-
aurus	Avonside Engine Co.	May 1869	-	0-6-0 ST	do	12½"x16"	2170	-
ing	do	Jan 1871	-	2-4-0 T	do	9"x16"	2171	-
rince	Ince Forge Co.	Jun 1871	-	do	4'0"	12"x17"	2137	-
sa	Avonside	(a)1863 (b)Jan 1868	-	0-6-0 ST*	4'6"	16½"x24"	2145	-
da	do	(a)1862 (b)Feb 1868	-	do	do	do	2146	-
a	do	(a)1862 (b)Apr 1868	-	do	do	do	2147	-
na	Rothwell & Co.	(a)1864 (b)Dec 1868	-	4-4-0 ST	5'3"**	17"x24"	2132	-
cla	do	(a)1864 (b)Dec 1872	-	do	5'3"**	do	2133	-
ron	Sharp Stewart & Co.	(a)1861 (b)Sep 1872	-	do	do	do	2134	-
gpie	do	(a)1861 (b)Sep 1872	-	do	do	do	2135	-
druth	West Cornwall Railway	(a)1865 (b)Dec 1871	-	0-6-0 ST	4'9"	do	2156	-
nwith	Stothert & Slaughter	(a)1853 (b)Jan 1872	-	2-4-0 T	5'0"	15"x22"	2136	-
lkeley	G.W.R. Swindon	(a)1865 (b)Aug 1872	Sir Watkin	0-6-0 T	4'6"	17"x24"	2157	-
wler	do	(a)1866 (b)Jul 1872	do	do	do	do	2158	-

*4-4-0 ST With 5'6" coupled wheels until 1874

**Later altered to 5'6" - possibly after acquired by G.W.R.

SCHEDULE of S.D.R. LOCO'S (Cont'd)

Name	Builder	(a) Date Built & (b) Date Acquired by S.D.R. if Different	Class	Type	Dimensions Driving Wheels	Cylinders	G.W.R. Broad Gauge No.	G.W.R. Narrow Gauge No.
(1)	(2)	(3)	(4)	(5)	(6)	(7)	(8)	(9)
Saunders	G.W.R. Swindon	(a)1866 (b)Jul 1872	Sir Watkin	0-6-0 T	4'6"	17"x24"	2159	-
Stromboli	do	(a)1852 (b)Sep 1872	-	0-6-0 ST	5'0"	do	2138	-
Buffalo	Avonside Engine Co.	Jun 1872	Buffalo	0-6-0 ST	4'9"	do	2160	1320
Elephant	do	Jul 1872	do	do	do	do	2161	1321
Camel	do	Aug 1872	do	do	do	do	2162	1322
Hercules	do	- do	do	do	do	do	2163	(withdrawn 1889)
Dragon	do	Sep 1873	do	do	do	do	2164	1323
Achilles	do	Dec 1873	do	do	do	do	2165	1324
Dromedary	do	do	do	do	do	do	2166	1325
Emperor	do	do	do	do	do	do	2167	1317
Python	do	Mar 1874	do	do	do	do	2168	1318
Vulcan	do	do	do	do	do	do	2169	1319
Leopard	do	Dec 1872	Leopard	4-4-0 ST	5'9"	do	2128	
Stag	do	do	do	do	do	do	2129	withdrawn June 1893
Lance	do	Feb 1875	do	do	do	do	2130	
Osiris	do	Mar 1875	do	do	do	do	2131	
Owl	do	Jan 1873	-	0-4-0 WT	3'0"	11"x16"	2172	1327
Weasel	Avonside Engine Co.	Mar 1873	-	0-4-0 WT	3'0"	11"x16"	2173	(withdrawn 1882)
Goat	do	Feb 1873	-	do	do	do	2174	1328
Raven	do	Nov 1874	-	0-4-0 ST	do	14"x18"*	2175	1329
Rook	do	do	-	do	do	do*	2176	1330
Crow	do	Dec 1874	-	do	do	do*	2177	1331
Lark	do	do	-	do	do	do*	2178	1332
Jay	do	Feb 1875	-	do	do	do*	2179	1333

*Some may have been fitted with 14"x17" cylinders

APPENDIX 3 — TABLE OF FASTEST EXPRESS TIMINGS 1846 TO 1982

Year	To or from Exeter				To or from Paddington				
	Journey	Distance	Time	Average MPH	Journey	Distance	Time	Average MPH	Notes
1846	To & from Teignmouth	15m.	0.45 m.	20	Down to Teignmouth	208¾m.	5hr 20m.	39.1	a
1848	To & from Laira Green	50m.	2hr 15m.	22.2	Down to Laira	243¾m.	6hr 55m.	35.2	a
1849	To & from Millbay	52¾m.	2hr 20m.	22.6	Down to Millbay	246½m.	7hr 05m.	34.8	a
1865	Down to Millbay	52¾m.	1hr 45m.	30.1	Down to Millbay	246½m.	6hr 30m.	37.9	a
1875	Down to Millbay	52¾m.	1hr 40m.	31.7	Down to Millbay	246½m.	6hr 10m.	40.0	a
1890	Down to North Road	52m.	1hr 30m.	34.7	Down to North Road	245¾m.	5hr 35m.	44.4	a
1901	Down to North Road	52m.	1hr 27m.	35.9	Down to North Road	245¾m.	5hr 0m.	49.1	ab
1904	Up from North Road	52m.	1hr 10m.	44.6	Up from North Road	245¾m.	4hr 25m.	55.6	ac
1906	} No Significant Improvements				Down to North Road	225¾m.	4hr 07m.	54.8	d
1927					Down to North Road	225¾m.	4hr 00m.	56.4	e
1964					Down to North Road	225¾m.	3hr 50m.	58.9	f
1968					Down to North Road	225¾m.	3hr 45m.	60.2	g
1969					Down to North Road	225¾m.	3hr 30m.	64.5	h
1982	To & from North Road	52m.	0.55m.	56.7	Down to North Road	225¾m.	3hr 04m.	73.6	i

Notes
a via Bristol
b Narrow Gauge
c Cornish Riviera Express; load limited to 5 bogies plus restaurant car
d Shorter route opened via Westbury
e 'King' class locos introduced
f diesel traction 'The Golden Hind'
g Load limited to 11 coaches
h Load limited to 9 coaches
i Inter-City 125 High Speed Train

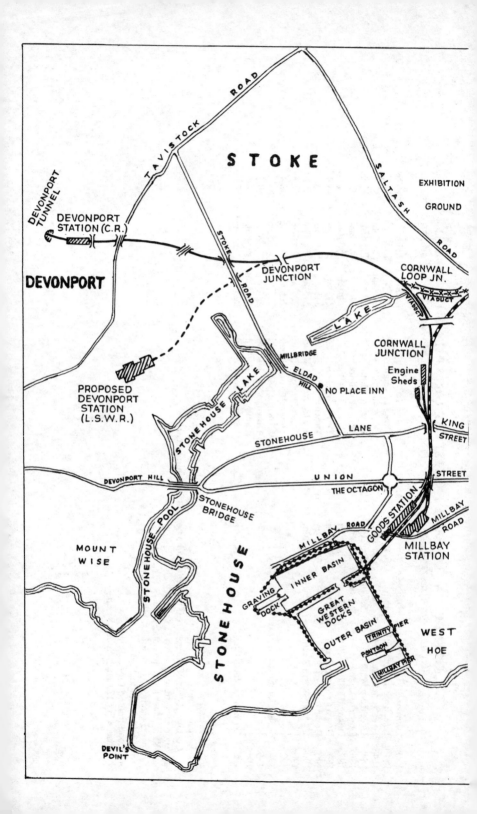

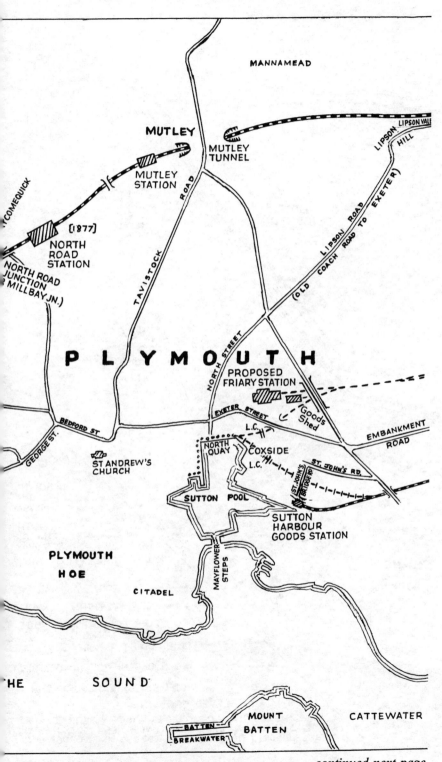

continued next page

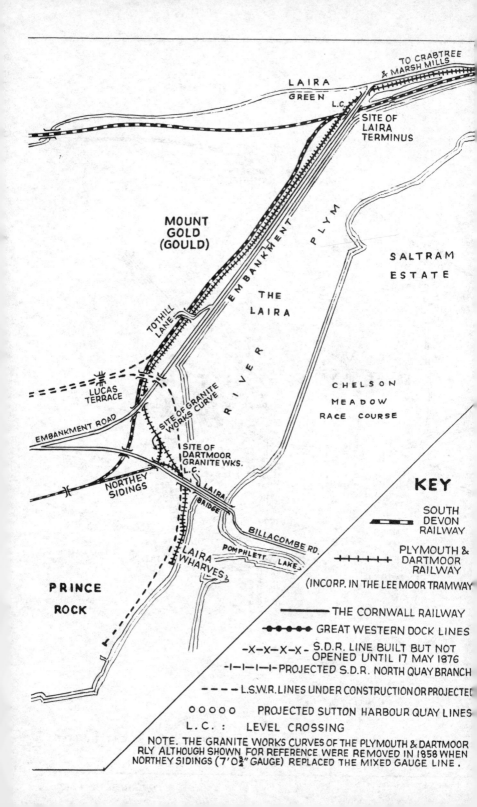

TO CRABTREE
& MARSH MILLS

LAIRA
GREEN
L.C.

SITE OF
LAIRA
TERMINUS

MOUNT
GOLD
(GOULD)

EMBANKMENT

PLYM

SALTRAM
ESTATE

THE
LAIRA

TOTHILL
LANE

RIVER

LUCAS
TERRACE

EMBANKMENT ROAD

SITE OF GRANITE
WORKS CURVE

CHELSON
MEADOW
RACE COURSE

SITE OF
DARTMOOR
GRANITE WKS.
L.C.

NORTHEY
SIDINGS

LAIRA
BRIDGE

KEY

BILLACOMBE RD.

POMPHLETT LAKE

LAIRA
WHARVES

SOUTH
DEVON
RAILWAY

PLYMOUTH &
DARTMOOR
RAILWAY

PRINCE
ROCK

(INCORP. IN THE LEE MOOR TRAMWAY

THE CORNWALL RAILWAY

●●●●● GREAT WESTERN DOCK LINES

-X-X-X-X- S.D.R. LINE BUILT BUT NOT
OPENED UNTIL 17 MAY 1876

-I-I-I-I- PROJECTED S.D.R. NORTH QUAY BRANCH

- - - - L.S.W.R. LINES UNDER CONSTRUCTION OR PROJECTED

OOOOO PROJECTED SUTTON HARBOUR QUAY LINES

L.C. : LEVEL CROSSING

NOTE. THE GRANITE WORKS CURVES OF THE PLYMOUTH & DARTMOOR
RLY ALTHOUGH SHOWN FOR REFERENCE WERE REMOVED IN 1858 WHEN
NORTHEY SIDINGS (7'0¾" GAUGE) REPLACED THE MIXED GAUGE LINE.

TIME TABLE.

Distance.	UP TRAINS.	On Week Days.								Sunday Trains.				Passenger Fares. Per Ordinary Trains.			Per Ordinary Trains to Exeter, & from thence, per Express	
		1st 2nd and 3rd Class	1st 2nd and 3rd Class			1st 2nd and 3rd Class								1st Class	2nd Class	3rd Class	1st Class	2nd Class
Miles	*Starting from*	a. m.	a. m.	a. m.	p. m.	p. m.	p. m.	p. m.	...	...	a. m.	a. m.	p. m.	s. d.	s. d.	s. d.	s. d.	s. d.
—	TEIGNMOUTH	7.10	9.10	11.10	1.15	4.25	6.45	8.45	...	...	7.15	9.3	8.30					
3	DAWLISH	7.19	9.19	11.19	1.24	4.34	6.54	8.54	..	...	7.24	9.39	8.41	0 6	0 4	0 3	0 6	0 4
6½	Starcross	7.30	9.30	11.30	1.25	4.45	7. 5	9. 5	...	...	7.35	9.50	8.55	1 0	0 9	0 6	1 0	0 9
15	EXETER, *Arrival*	7.55	9.55	11.55	2 0	5.10	7.30	9 30			8. 0	10.18	9.25	2 6	2 0	1 [illegible]	2 6	2 0
		1st & 2nd Class a. m.	1st & 2nd Class a. m.	Express train noon.	Day Mail 1st. p m			MAIL p m.					MAIL. p. m.					
15	EXETER, *Departure per Great Western Train*	8 0	10. 0	12. 0	3.15	5 15	...	9 35	...	...	...	...	9.35	—	—	—	—	—
23½	Hele	8 15	10.15	...	3 31	5.33	...	...	...	...	...	...	...	4 6	3 0	2 6	—	—
27¾	CULLUMPTON	8.26	10.24	...	3 39	5 42	...	9 57	...	...	...	...	9.57	5 6	3 6	2 4	—	—
29¾	TIVERTON ROAD	8.34	10.30	...	3 44	5 48	...	10. 1	...	...	...	...	10. 1	6 0	4 0	2 6	—	—
38¾	WELLINGTON	8.54	10 51	...	4 3	6 13	...	10.23	...	...	...	...	10.23	8 0	5 6	3 3	—	—
45½	TAUNTON	9.10	11. 7	12.41	4 17	6.30	...	10.40	...	...	...	...	10.40	10 0	6 6	3 10	11 6	7 6
57½	BRIDGEWATER	9.30	11.28	...	4.37	6.55	..	11. 5	...	..	..	...	11. 5	12 6	8 8	4 10	—	—
63½	HIGHBRIDGE, near Burnham	9.45	...	...	4.50	7. 6	..	...	...	...	...	...	...	14 0	9 0	5 4	—	—
73½	WESTON SUPER MARE *Junction*	9.50	11 48	...	4 58	7.10	...	...	...	...	...	...	...	15 6	10 6	6 2	—	—
75	Banwell	...	12 4	...	...	7.32	...	...	...	...	...	...	...	16 0	11 0	6 3	—	—
78½	CLEVEDON ROAD, Yatton	10 12	12.11	...	5.20	7 42	...	...	...	...	...	...	...	17 0	12 0	6 7	—	—
82½	Nailsea	...	..	...	5 30	7 52	...	...	..	...	...	...	...	18 0	12 6	6 11	—	—
90½	BRISTOL .. *Arrival*	10 40	12.35	1.36	5.50	8 15	...	12.15	...	...	...	...	12.15	20 0	13 6	7 7	22 6	15 0
	Departure	10.50	12 45	1.41	6 0	8 30	...	12.25	...	...	...	...	12 25	—	—	—	—	—
102	BATH	11.18	1.10	1.56	6.25	9. 0	...	12.45	...	...	...	...	12.45	22 6	15 0	8 6	25 0	16 6
115	CHIPPENHAM	11.50	1.41	...	7.10	9 38	...	1.15	..	...	...	...	1.15	25 6	17 6	9 7	—	—
131¾	SWINDON ... *Arrival*	12 20	2.15	2.43	7.40	10.15	...	1.50	...	...	..	...	1.50	29 6	20 0	11 0	33 0	22 0
	Departure	12.36	2.25	2.53	7 50	...	..	2. 0	...	...	...	...	2. 0	—	—	—	—	—
155¾	DIDCOT	1.19	3.27	3 22	8 33	...	..	2.49	...	..	...	...	2.49	35 0	24 0	13 0	39 6	27 6
173	READING	2. 0	4.10	...	9.13	...	...	3.30	...	...	...	...	3 30	39 0	26 6	14 5	—	—
186¼	MAIDENHEAD	...	4 30	...	9.42	..	...	4. 0	...	...	...	...	4. 0	42 0	27 6	15 7	—	—
190¾	SLOUGH	2.40	4.45	..	9.50	...	...	4 10	...	...	...	...	4.10	43 0	29 6	15 11	—	—
208¾	PADDINGTON	3.20	5.30	4.30	10 50	...	..	4.50	...	..	...	...	4 50	47 0	33 0	17 5	52 6	36 0

Distance.	DOWN TRAINS.	On Week Days.								Sunday Trains				Passenger Fares. per Ordinary Trains.			per Express Trains.	
				Express Train.				*Express Train.*				Day Mail to Bstl.		1st Class	2nd Class	3rd Class	1st Class	2nd Class
Miles	*Starting from*	...	..	a. m.	a. m.	a. m.	noon.	p. m.				a. m	p. m.	s d	s d	s d	s d	s d
—	PADDINGTON *per Gt. Western Tr.*	...	..	9 45	7 30	10 15	12 0	5 30	...	...	...	10 15	2 0	—	—	—	—	—
18	SLOUGH	...	...	...	8. 5	10 53	12 38	..	...	...	...	10 52	2 40	4 0	2 6	1 6	—	—
22½	MAIDENHEAD	...	...	...	8.18	11 3	...	..	...	...	...	11 3	2 52	5 0	3 6	1 11	—	—
35¾	READING	..	..	...	8.48	11 35	1 20	6 13	...	...	...	11 35	3 21	8 0	5 6	3 0	8 6	6 0
53	DIDCOT	...	...	10.50	9.38	12 12	2 0	...	...	...	..	12 12	4 3	12 0	8 0	4 5	13 0	8 6
77	SWINDON *Arrival*	...	...	11.23	10 30	1 5	2 55	7 8	...	...	...	1 5	5 0	17 6	12 0	6 5	20 0	14 0
	Departure	...	...	11 33	10.40	1 15	3 5	7 18	...	...	...	1 15	5 10	—	—	—	—	—
93¾	CHIPPENHAM	..	...	...	11.18	1 45	3 30	7 37	...	...	...	1 45	5 45	21 6	14 6	7 10	24 6	17 6
106¾	BATH	...	..	12. 9	11.53	2 10	3 58	7 55	...	...	...	2 10	6 18	24 6	17 0	8 11	27 6	19 6
118¼	BRISTOL *Arrival*	...	...	12.28	12.18	2 35	4 25	8 15	...	...	...	2 35	6 48	27 0	18 6	9 11	30 0	21 0
	Departure	..	...	12.33	12 40	2 45	4 55	8 18	...	...	...	2 55	7 5	—	—	—	—	—
126¼	Nailsea	...	...	...	12.58	...	4 53	...	...	...	...		7 23	20 0	19 6	10 7	—	—
130¼	CLEVEDON ROAD, Yatton	...	...	...	1. 8	3 13	5 3	...	...	...	..	3 2[illegible]	7 32	30 0	20 0	10 11	—	—
133¾	Banwell	...	...	...	...	...	5 13	...	...	...	...	...	7 40	31 0	21 0	11 2	—	—
136¾	WESTON SUPER MARE *Junction*	...	...	...	1.18	3 31	5 21	...	...	...	...	3 35	7 49	31 6	21 6	11 7	—	—
145¼	HIGHBRIDGE, near Burnham	...	...	...	...	3 49	5 41	...	...	...	...	3 53	8 7	33 0	23 0	12 2	—	—
151¼	BRIDGEWATER	..	...	..	1 50	4 3	5 55	8 57	...	...	..	4 10	8 24	34 6	23 6	12 8	38 0	26 6
163	TAUNTON	..	...	1.29	2 15	4 23	6 22	9 17	...	...	...	4 30	8 45	37 0	25 6	13 7	41 0	28 6
170	WELLINGTON	...	...	..	...	4 40	6 39	...	.	...	...	4 45	9 0	39 0	26 6	14 2	—	—
179	TIVERTON ROAD	...	...	...	2 45	5 0	7 0	..	...	...	...	5 5	9 25	41 0	28 0	14 11	—	—
181½	CULLUMPTON	...	...	...	2 50	..	7 7	...	...	...	...	5 10	9 32	41 6	28 6	15 2	—	—
18[illegible]	Hele	...	...	...	3 0	5 15	7 17	...	...	...	...	5 20	9 42	42 6	29 0	15 6	—	—
193¾	EXETER. *Arrival*	...	...	2.15	3 20	5 32	7 35	10 5	...	...	...	5 35	10 0	44 6	30 0	16 2	50 0	34 0
		1st 2nd & 3rd Class a. m.				1st 2nd & 3rd Class	1st 2nd & 3rd Class p m.				a. m.						Per Ordinary Trains below Exeter.	
193¾	EXETER. *Departure per South Devon Train*	8.10	12.10	2.20	3 25	5 40	7 40	10 10	...	...	8 20	5 40	10 5	—	—	—	—	—
202¼	Starcross	8.35	12.35	2 45	3.50	6 5	8 5	10 35	...	..	8 50	6 5	10 30	46 0	31 3	16 11	51 6	35 3
205¾	DAWLISH	8.46	12.46	2.56	4 1	6 16	8 16	10 46	...	..	9 4	6 16	10 41	46 6	31 8	17 2	52 0	35 8
208¾	TEIGNMOUTH	8 55	12.55	3. 5	4.10	6 25	8 25	10 55	...	...	9 15	6 25	10 50	47 0	32 0	17 5	52 6	36 0

PASSENGERS' LUGGAGE. — First Class Passengers are allowed 112 lbs. of Luggage; and Second and Third Class Passengers are allowed 60 lbs. free of charge. All excess is charged for according to distance.

COACHES or OMNIBUSES run from Teignmouth to Newton, Ashburton, Totnes, Ivybridge, Plympton, Plymouth, Devonport, Falmouth, Torquay, Paignton, Brixham, Dartmouth, &c.

RETURN TICKETS.—NOTICE—First or Second Class Passengers paying the Fare for a Return Ticket will be allowed a reduction of one-third on the double Journey, subject to the following conditions:—The Return Ticket is on no account to be transferred to any Passenger. A portion of the Ticket will be cut off, on being exhibited at the completion of the first Journey. Upon the return Journey, the passenger must show the Ticket, in the Booking-office of the Station to have it re-stamped by the Clerk, before he enters the carriage, without which it will not be received.

Return Tickets will only be available as under:—For a distance not exceeding 60 miles, on the same day. Not exceeding 120 miles, on the same or the next day (Sundays not being counted). Exceeding 120 miles, on the same, or either of the two next days (Sundays not being counted). If the Return Ticket be not used within the prescribed period, it will be no longer available, and the extra amount paid for it will be forfeited.

The original time-table operated from 30 May 1846.

EXTRACTS FROM WORKING TIME-TABLES DEC. 1875

2

NOTICES.

Particular attention is requested to the following :—

This Book is issued for the use and information of the Companies Servants only.

Each Station Master is desired to examine and compare the working Time Books and Passenger Time Bills, as often as they are issued, so far as his own Station is concerned, and to report immediately any inaccuracies he may discover, to the Superintendent of the Line.

If an Engineman refuse to take on Trucks from any Station, it will be the duty of the Station Master, or person in authority, to report the case to the Superintendent of the Line.

Should a Goods Train, on arriving at a Station, be so heavily laden that it cannot take on more loaded Waggons, the Guard is to ascertain what Traffic there is to be forwarded, and if it is Perishable, Market, or General Goods, he is to detach from his Train a sufficient number of mileage or empty Waggons, so that the Traffic which is urgent may be taken on.

Every exertion must be made by the Goods Guards for the Trains under their charge to arrive at the Stations where they are marked to "Shunt" at the times fixed.

As from unavoidable causes, such as the arrival of connecting Trains from other Lines, the weather, state of the rails, the loads to be conveyed, the business to be transacted, and other varying circumstances, the Goods Trains are liable to be late in starting, and must on the journey be subject also to detention, in consequence of waiting for Passenger Trains to pass: the times are given for the guidance of the Servants of the Companies, so that they may not allow a Goods Train to leave any Station BEFORE the appointed time.

When an Up Train, which is not appointed to stop at Dawlish, has to cross a Down Goods Train at that Station, the Down Goods Train must not be admitted below the Down Line distant signal until the Up Train has passed upon the Up Line.

Drivers and Guards must strictly observe the following Regulations :—

No Passenger, Goods, or Special Train is to run through any Station between Penzance and Truro at a greater speed than 8 miles per hour.

Up Trains from West Cornwall must not pass over the Penwither's Junction Points at a greater speed than 8 miles per hour.

All Narrow Guage, and Mixed Narrow and Broad Guage Goods Trains, must stop dead at all Stations between Truro and Penzance.

Goods Trains must be stopped dead at the following places:

ON THE UP JOURNEY AT	ON THE DOWN JOURNEY AT
Devonport	Marsh Mills
Rattery	Hemerdon
Dainton (entrance to Tunnel)	West end of Mutley Tunnel
	Summit of Incline near Falmouth

The Guards must (if necessary), at the places named put down a sufficient number of Breaks to ensure their Trains being well under control. The Guards must satisfy themselves that the Breaks are in good condition. They should be so applied that the Wheels may rub tightly against the Break Blocks without allowing the Wheels to skid. Spraggs must never be applied to the Wheels of Trucks if there are sufficient Breaks to control the Trains.

The Total number of Trucks allowed in any one Goods Train.

FROM	TO	IS
Tavistock	Plymouth	28
Hemerdon	Plymouth	28
Plymouth	Penryn	30
Penryn	Falmouth	25

When Trucks are left behind by reason of the weight of the Train, the particulars must be reported by Telegraph to the Superintendent of the Line with the least possible delay.

N.B.—The speed of Goods Trains running between Exeter and Newton must not exceed 30 miles per hour, and over any other part of the system, 25 miles per hour.

☞ **When a Train has to cross another Train at a Station at which it is not appointed to Stop, the Driver of the Train which is not appointed to stop must approach the Distance Signal at reduced speed, and when the Signal is showing "All Right," pass through the Station slowly, and be prepared to stop at it by hand signal or otherwise.**

IMPORTANT NOTICE TO ENGINE DRIVERS.

The Main Lines and Branches are worked under the "Block" system of Telegraph, that is to say: no Train may be allowed to pass any Station, or Signal Box, until the previous Train has passed within the Signals of the next Station, or Signal Box, in advance; and it must be specially noted that the "All Right" Signal given at any one Station, or Signal Box, only denotes that the Line is clear up to the Distant Signal of the next Station, or Signal Box, and not within it. Engine Drivers must, therefore, always keep their Trains under such control as to be able to stop at each Signal.

NOTICE TO DRIVERS AND GOODS GUARDS.

When the Signals which protect the following Sidings, stand at danger, Detonators (fixed on an iron rod attached to the base of the Signals) will be placed on the Line of rails, which the Signals govern. When Drivers run over the Detonators, they must stop their Trains as speedily as possible.

MAIN LINE.

East Cliff (between Dawlish and Teignmouth)............	Down Signal.
Cornwood	Up "
Bodennick Siding (between Grampound Road and Burngullow)	Up "
Trenance Siding (between Burngullow and St. Austell)...........	Down "
Par Harbour (between St. Austell and Par)..........................	Down "
Glynn Valley Siding (between Bodmin Road and Doublebois)...	Up "

TORQUAY BRANCH.

Gas House Siding (between Torquay and Paignton)................	Up "

MORETONHAMPSTEAD BRANCH.

Sandrick Wood Siding (between Moreton and Lustleigh)........ ..	Up "
Granite and Pottery Sidings (between Bovey and Teigngrace)....	Up "
Teigngrace..	Up "

TAVISTOCK AND LAUNCESTON BRANCH.

Lifton Quarry Siding (between Launceston and Lifton).	Up "
Leat Siding (between Launceston and Lifton)...........................	Up "
Brentor Siding (between Lidford and Mary Tavy).	Up "
Yelverton Siding (between Horrabridge and Bickleigh).............	Up & Down Signals
Shaugh Siding (between Horrabridge and Bickleigh).................	Up Signal.

NOTICE

TO STATION MASTERS, FOREMEN, and SHUNTING PORTERS, GOODS GUARDS, and other SERVANTS of the COMPANIES.

Goods Trains must be Formed as follows, and the Guards must report every case in which the instructions are not strictly carried out:—

FORMING GOODS TRAINS

These Trains must be so formed that all the Waggons for each Station shall be together, and particular care must be taken to arrange them in consecutive order, according to distance. This order must be observed throughout the journey, until the Waggons reach their destination.

All Traffic for the longest distances must have the preference.

INVOICES.

The Guards must see that they have Invoices for all the Waggons in their Trains, and they must report every instance in which this Rules is departed from. Great care must be observed to prevent the Invoices being over-carried, or given out at any point other than the proper one.

PRIVATE WAGGONS.

Empty private Waggons not having proper addresses upon them, must be labelled home (in the absence of instructions) and, if going to a foreign Line, the route must be stated on the Truck label.

Distances.	STATIONS.	1 GOODS	2 Goods.	3 Goods.	4 Passenger.	5 Passenger.	6 Passenger.	7 Passenger.	8 N.G. Goods.	9 Passenger.	10 Passenger.
—	Penzance dep.	...	...	...	...	.	...	...	...	a.m. *8 10	...
2	Marazion Road	...	...	...	...	...	...	...	...	8 16	...
5¾	St. Ives Road...	...	...	...	...	...	...	...	...	8 25	...
7¼	Hayle	...	...	...	...	...	...	...	...	8 31	...
10¾	Gwinear Rd. ...	...	...	...	...	...	...	...	...	8 41	...
13¼	Camborne ...	..	...	...	...	...	...	...	...	†8 49	...
14¾	Carn Brea ...	...	...	...	...	...	...	...	...	8 55	...
—	Carn Brea Yard	...	...	...	...	...	...	...	a.m. 7 24	...	...
16½	Redruth ...	...	...	...	...	...	...	...	7 40	9 2	...
18¾	Scorrier Gate ...	...	...	...	...	...	...	...	§7 50	9 9	...
20¾	Chacewater ...	...	...	...	...	...	...	...	7 58	9 15	...
—	Newham ...	...	...	..	...	...	...	...	8 15	...	...
26	Truro .. arr.	..	...	...	.	..	...	...		*9 27	...
—	Falmouth dep.	..	...	..	..	...	..	a.m. 6 20	..	8 50	...
3¼	Penryn ...	...	...	...	...	...	...	6 29	...	†9 0	...
7½	Perranwell ...	...	...	...	...	...	...	6 38	...	9 10	...
11¾	Truro arr.	...	...	...	...	...	...	6 47	...	9 20	...
—	Truro dep.	..	...	..	..	...	..	7 20	...	9 33	...
33½	Grampound Rd.	...	...	...	...	...	...	7 37	...	9 50	...
38¼	Burngullow ...	...	...	...	...	...	...	†7 48	...	10 1	...
40¼	St. Austell ...	...	...	...	...	...	...	7 54	...	10 8	...
45	Par	...	...	...	...	...	...	8 4	...	10 18	...
49¼	Lostwithiel ...	...	...	...	...	...	...	*8 18	...	10 31	...
52¾	Bodmin Rd. ...	...	..	...	...	...	...	†8 28	Engine & Empty Carriages.	10 40	...
58½	Doublebois ...	...	...	...	...	...	...	8 45		10 57	...
61¾	Liskeard ...	...	...	...	...	...	...	8 55		11 7	...
64¾	Menheniot ...	...	...	...	...	...	...	9 4		11 16	...
70¼	St. Germans ...	...	...	...	...	a.m.	...	9 16		*11 28	...
75¼	Saltash ...	...	...	...	...	8 0	...	9 29		11 42	...
78¼	Devonport ...	...	...	...	...	8 8	...	9 38		11 51	...
79¾	Plymouth arr.	A F	A	A B		8 15	...	9 45		12 0	...
—	Plymouth dep.	a.m. 12 15	a.m. 4 30	a.m. 5 35	a.m. 6 35	a.m. 8 35	a.m. 9 5	a.m. 10 0	a.m. 8 40	p.m. 12 20	...
80¾	Mutley ...	12 20	4 35	5 40	6 40	8 39	9 10	10 4	8 44	12 28	...
—	Laira	12 40	4 40	5 50	...	..	...	...	...	...	..
84½	Plympton ...	1 20	4 50	6 0	6 52	8 45	9 20	10 9	8 52	12 38	...
88¾	Cornwood ...	1 40	5 20	6 35	7 7	8 54	9 36	10 19		12 56	...
91¼	Ivybridge ...	1 50	5 30	§6 55	†7 14	†8 59	9 42	*10 26	...	1 2	...
94½	Kingsbridge Rd	2 0	5 45	‡7 30	‡7 22	*9 5	9 50	†10 32	...	1 10	...
96¾	Brent		5 55	7 50	7 30	9 10	†9 58	10 37	...	1 18	...
103½	Totnes	..	6 20	8 30	7 48	9 23	10 15	10 50	...	1 35	...
—	Torquay Junc.	.	...	...	...	...	...	...	...	...	...
112¼	Newton arr.	...	7 20	9 20	8 10	9 40	10 38	11 8	...	1 58	...
	Newton dep.	...	7 45	‡10 0	8 20	‡9 44	10 43	11 13	...	2 3	...
117½	Teignmouth ..	...	8 10	†‡11 5	8 33	9 56	‡*1055	11 25	...	2 15	...
120¼	Dawlish ..	...	8 22	‡§1150	8 44	10 6	†11 5	‡11†36	...	2 25	...
124	Starcross ...	...	8 34	12 15	8 54	10 12	11 15	11 50	...	2 36	...
127¾	Exminster ...	...	8 45	C.R.	9 4	10 17	11 25	11 58	...	2 46	...
131	St Thomas ...	...	8 56	C.B.	9 18	10 23	11 35	12 7	...	3 0	...
132	Exeter arr.	...	9 0	12 55	9 25	10 25	11 40	12 10	...	3 5	...
—	Exeter dep.	...	p.m. 12 30	p.m. 4 50	a.m. 9 45	a.m. 10 30	...	p.m. 12 18	...	3 20	...
208	Bristol arr.	...	4 15	10 12	1 5	12 4	...	2 35	..	6 25	...
26¼	Paddington arr.	...	a.m. 12 45	...	5 15	2 45	...	6 0	..	..	...

A These Trains will not run on Mondays. B If it be necessary to divide this Train on the Dainton Incline part of it may be sent to the Siding at Dainton immediately on arrival of the Train at Totnes, provided that doing so no up Train be delayed at Totnes.

F This Train must not foul the Main Line at Plympton until after the Down 7.30 p.m. Goods Train has passed.

	11	12	13	14	15	16	17	18	19	20	21
STATIONS.	N.G. GOODS.	Passenger.	Passenger and Perishable Goods.	N.G. GOODS.	N.G. GOODS.	GOODS.	Passenger	B.G. Goods.	Mixed GOODS.	Passenger.	
		a.m.	a.m.			p.m.	p.m.		p.m.	p.m.	
Penzance dep...	...	10 0	11 15	...	...	1 15	3 50	...	3 15	6 30	...
Marazion Road	...	†10 6	11 21	...	...	1 45	3 56	...	3 30	6 36	...
St. Ives Road	a.m.	10 15	11 31	p.m.	p.m.	2 0	4 5	...	3 45	6 45	...
Hayle ...	8 45	*10 22	11 38	1 10	4 40	†2 32	‡4 12	...	‡4 25	*6 51	...
Gwinear Rd. ...	§8 59	10 32	†11 48	1 25	4 55	†2 52	4 22	...	4 40	7 1	...
Camborne ...	9 10	10 40	†11 58	1 40	5 10	3 25	4 30	...	5 5	7 7	...
Carn Brea ...	9 20	10 46	12 3	1 50	5 20	3 35	4 36	...	5 10	7 13	...
Carn Brea Yard	9 30	...	...	1 55	5 25	...	...	...	...	...	...
Redruth ...	...	†10 53	12 12	...	...	4 0	4 43	...	5 36	7 19	...
Scorrier Gate ...	...	11 0	12 20	...	...	4 10	4 50	...	6 0	7 27	...
Chacewater ...	...	11 6	12 26	...	...	4 20	4 56	...	†6 8	7 34	...
Newham ...	...	...	...	...	...	...	...	...	...	...	...
Truro　arr.	...	11 18	12 40	B.G. Goods	...	‡4 40	‡5 8	...	6 20	7 51	...
Falmouth dep.	B.G. GOODS.	10 45	...	...	...	...	4 35	4 45	...	7 20	...
Penryn ...		10 55	...	...	...	...	4 45	5 10	...	7 30	...
Perranwell ...		11 5	...	...	...	...	4 55	5 30	...	7 40	...
Truro　arr.		11 15	...	...	...	...	5 5	5 50	...	7 50	...
			p.m.	p.m.							
Truro　dep.	...	11 28	12 50	...	B.G. GOODS	†5 55	5 15	†6 50	7 45	...	...
Grampound Rd.	p.m.	11 45	*1 9	6 55		6 24	*5 32	C.R.	†8 19	...	...
Burngullow ...	1 30	11 58	1 18	‡‡†9 0		6 52	5 42	‡†8 8	‡8 40	...	...
St. Austell ...	1 45	†12 4	1 27	9 30		7 0	5 47	8 46	9 15	...	WEDNESDAYS ONLY.
Par ...	2 15	12 14	1 39	10 0	p.m.	7 25	5 57	9 5	9 40	...	
Lostwithiel ...	2 35	*12 27	1 55		3 30	†7 38	6 9	9 35	10 10	...	
Bodmin Rd. ...	...	12 36	2 7		3 45	7 48	6 18	9 45	10 35	...	
Doublebois ...	...	12 53	2 24		†4 23	8 30	6 35	10 10	11 15	...	
Liskeard ...	...	1 4	2 39		5 14	†8 50	6 45	10 20	12§10	p.m.	
Menheniot ...	...	1 13	2 47		5 31	9 0	*6 54	10 35	12 30	9 5	
St. Germans ...	...	1 27	2 59		6 0	9 12	7 7	10§55	12 55	9 14	
Saltash ...	...	1 41	3 13		†6 25	9 24	7 19	11 20	1 15	9 26	p.m.
Devonport ...	...	1 51	3 22		6 45	9 40	7 27	11 40	1 35	9 38	11 20
Plymouth arr.	...	2 0	*3 30	Passenger.	7 5	9 45	7 35	11 50	1 50	9 47	11 28
		p.m.	p.m.	p.m.			p.m.	p.m.	p.m.	9 55	11 35
Plymouth dep.	...	2 15	4 1)	6 0	...	...	7 45	8 15	9 15	..	Gds. E 11 30
Mutley ..	...	2 19	4 1|	6 5	...	...	7 49	8 20	9 20	...	11 35
Laira ...	...	...	...	...	...	...	...	8 40	9 30	...	11 40
Plympton ...	...	2 27	4 22	6 15	...	...	7 57	8 50	9 40	...	11 50
Cornwood ...	...	2 40	4 37	6 31	...	...	8 10	9 23	10 8	...	12 10
Ivybridge ...	...	2 46	4 44	6 37	...	...	8 15	9 33	10 18	...	12§30
Kingsbridge Rd.	...	†2 55	4 54	6 45	...	...	8 23	10 0	10 30	...	12 45
Brent ...	..	3 1	5 2	*6 54	...	...	8 25	10 10	10 40	...	12 55
Totnes ...	..	3 15	5 18	7 12	...	...	8 42	10 35	11 15	...	1 25
Torquay Junc.	...	...	...	...	...	...	...	...	...	...	...
Newton { arr.	...	3 33	5 40	7 34	...	...	†9 3	11 15	11 55	...	2 10
Newton { dep.	...	3 43	5 48	7 43	...	...	9 10	11 45	12 30	...	§3 25
Teignmouth ...	...	3 55	6 1	7 55	...	...	9 22	12 5	12 50	...	4 5
Dawlish ...	...	4 5	6 12	†8 5	...	...	9 32	12 16	1 2	...	4 40
Starcross ...	...	4 15	6 22	8 15	...	...	9 42	12 34	1 15	...	4 53
Exminster ...	...	4 23	6 32	8 25	...	...	9 49	12 46	1 27	...	5 5
St. Thomas ...	...	4 30	6 45	8 35	...	...	9 57	12 59	1 40	...	5 17
Exeter　arr.	...	4 35	6 50	8 40	...	...	10 2	1 5	1 45	...	5 20
								a.m.	a.m.		a.m
Exeter　dep.	..	4 45	7 10	Kent, Fish, and Perishable Goods.	..	..	10 12	4 0	4 0	...	8 10
Bristol .. arr.	..	6 45	10 45		..	..	12 32	10 15	10 15	...	2 0
Paddington arr.	...	10 20	3 30 C		...	...	4 35	4 45	4 45	...	...

ᴇ This Train must leave Saltash before the 4.45 p.m Up Goods Train.
C On Saturdays this Train does not run beyond Bristol.

Down Trains.

Distances.	STATIONS.	1 Goods.	2 Goods.	3 Passenger.	4 Passenger.	5 Goods.	6 Passenger.	7 Goods.	8 Passenger.	9 GOODS	10
—	Paddington dep	..	..	...	p.m. 8 10	...	..	p.m. 11 10		...	...
118¼	Bristol .. dep.	..	p.m. 6 5	..	a.m. 12 30	p.m. 9 50	..	4 0	a.m. 6 15	a.m. 12 45	...
193¾	Exeter arr.	..	11 25	...	2 50	2 20	..	6 35	8 27	6 10	
			C D			C D					...
—	Exeter dep.	...	a.m. 1 0	...	a.m. 3 0	a.m. 4 0	a.m. 7 5	a.m. 6 45	a.m. 8 40	a.m 9 0	...
194¾	St. Thomas ...	...	1 4	...	3 2	C.R.	7 15	6 47	8 45	C.R.	...
198½	Exminster ...	...	1 17	...	3 7	C.R.	7 24	6 55	8 52	C R.	...
202¼	Starcross ...	...	1 32	...	3 13	4 55	7 33	7 3	9 1	9 45	...
206	Dawlish ...	...	1 43	...	3 18	5 15	7 43	7 11	9 11	§†11‡36	† ..
208¾	Teignmouth ...	...	2 15	...	3 25	5 42	7 53	7 19	9 21	12 0	...
214	Newton arr.	..	§2 35	...	3 34	6 0	8 5	7 30	9 33	12 20	...
	Newton dep.	...	‡3 55	..	‡3 42	6 45	8 10	7 40	9 38	12 45	...
—	Torquay Junc.	...	...	...	...	...	...	...	..	...	...
222¾	Totnes ..	...	5 30	...		‡‡ 8 50	‡8 35	‡8 0	9 58	‡1 55	...
229½	Brent ...	C a.m.	6 30	...	3 57	†9 58	8 56	8 30	10 15	2 40	...
231½	Kingsbridge Rd	2 30	6 45	...	4 11	†‡10 35	*9 5	8 40	‡10 19	†2 53	...
235	Ivybridge ...	2 50	†§7 14	...	4 14	C.R.	9 15	†8 59	*10 26	3 15	...
237¼	Cornwood ...	3 5	7 25	a.m.	4 18	C.R.	9 21	9 4	10 30	C.R.	...
241¾	Plympton ...	3 30	C.R.	9 0	4 22	C.R.	9 35	9 17	10 37	C.R.	...
—	Laira ...	3 50	7 50	...	4 28	C.R.	...	9 23	...	C.R.	...
—	Mutley ...	4 0	8 15	9 10	... 4 37	11 20	9 45	9 30	10 45	3 30	...
246½	Plymouth arr.	4 5	8 20	9 18	4 40	11 25	9 55	9 35	10 48	4 0	...
—	Plymouth dep.	C a.m 2 0	C a.m. 3 30	a.m. 5 15	a.m. 4 50	a.m 7 35	a.m. 6 50	...	a m 11 0	...	...
248	Devonport ...	2 10	3 35	5 30	4 53	7 40	6 56	...	11 6	...	...
250¾	Saltash ...	2 20	3 50	5 50	5 1	7 50	7 4	...	11 14	...	...
256	St. Germans ...	C.R.	C.R.	6 15	5 12	Passenger Train	7 18	...	*11 28	...	...
261¼	Menheniot ...	C.R.	C.R.	6 40	5 23		7 32	...	11 42	...	...
264½	Liskeard ...	3 15	4 45	7 20	5 30		7 42	...	11 52	...	...
267½	Doublebois ...	C.R.	C.R.	‡8 12	5 36		‡7 52	B.G.	12 2	...	...
274¼	Bodmin Road	3 50	‡6 0	†8 28	‡5 49		8 8	Goods a.m	12 17	...	..
277	Lostwithiel ...	4 10	6 20	8 50	5 56		*8 18	10 55	12*27	...	...
281¼	Par	4 30	6 45		6 5		8 30	11 15	12 39	...	...
285½	St. Austell ...	5 0	7 15	GOODS.	6 15		8 43	†12 4	12 52	...	...
287¾	Burngullow ...	C.R.	†7 48		6 19		8 49	12 20	12 57	...	...
292¾	Grampound Rd.	5 45	8 29		6 29		9 1		*1 9	...	...
300¼	Truro .. arr.	‡6 15	9 0		‡6 45		9 18	...	1 26	...	...
—	Truro .. dep.	7 45	..	..	6 50	...	9 30	...	1 35	...	...
4	Perranwell ...	8 15	...		6 57	...	9 40	...	1 45	...	...
8¼	Penryn ...	†9 0	B .G.	N.G.	7 5	...	9 50	...	1 55	...	...
11¾	Falmouth arr.	9 20	Goods	Goods	7 15	...	10 0	...	2 5	..	...
—	Truro .. dep.	...	a.m. 10 0		‡6 53	...	a.m. *9 27	...	p.m 1 32	...	...
—	Newham ...	N.G. Goods	...	a.m. 9 40	..	N.G. Goods	...	N.G. Goods	...	...	...
305½	Chacewater ...	...	10 25	10 0	7 5	...	9 39	...	1 48	...	...
307½	Scorrier Gate ...	...	10 35	10 10	7 10	a.m.	9 44	...	1 54	...	...
309¾	Redruth ...	a.m.	†11 5	10 20	7 18	...	9 52	p.m	2 2	...	...
—	Carn Brea Yard	7 30	...	10 30	...	11 0	...	2 15	...	...	...
311½	Carn Brea ...	7 36	11 15	...	7 24	11 5	9 58	2 20	2 8	...	...
313	Camborne ...	7 46	11†58	...	7 31	11 13	10 5	2 40	2 15	...	...
315½	Gwinear Road	7 56	12 8	...	7 39	†11 48	10 13	†2 52	2 23	...	...
319	Hayle ...	8 10	12 25	...	7 48	11 58	10*22	3 5	†2 32	...	...
320½	St. Ives Road ...		12 35	...	7 54		10 28		2 38	...	...
324¼	Marazion Road	...	1 0	...	8 4	..	10 38	...	2 47	...	...
326¼	Penzance arr.	...	1 5	...	*8 10	...	10 44		2 53	...	..

C These Trains will not run on Mondays

D If these Trains have to divide on Rattery Incline the first part of the Trains may be sent to Rattery immediately on their arrival at Totnes, but they must be clear in Rattery Siding before the following Down Train is due to leave Totnes. The Engines will return to Totnes on the Up Line, after Line clear has been obtained from that Station.

STATIONS.	11 Passenger	12 Passenger.	13 Passenger.	14 Passenger.	15 Passenger.	16 Passenger.	17 Passenger.	18 Goods.	19 Passenger.	20	21
Paddington dep	..	a.m. 5 30	a.m. 9 0	·	a.m. 11 45	..	a.m. 10 30	a.m. 12 35	p.m. 5 0	...	...
Bristol ... dep.	...	9 15	p.m. 12 10	...	p.m. 2 26	...	p.m. 3 15	9 55	8 15	...	...
Exeter arr.	...	11 55	2 21	...	4 0	...	6 43	p.m. 3 30	10 20	...	...
								F D			
Exeter dep.	a.m. 10 10	p.m. 12 10	p.m. 2 30	...	p.m. 4 10	p.m. 5 10	p.m. 6 55	p.m. 7 30	p.m. 10 25	...	...
St. Thomas ...	10 15	12 18	2 35	...	4 12	5 17	7 2	7 34	10 27	...	...
Exminster ...	10 25	12 29	2 43	...	4 18	5 26	7 11	7 45	10 38	...	...
Starcross ..	10 35	12 39	2 53	...	4 24	5 35	7 20	7 57	10 40	...	...
Dawlish ...	‡10 45	12 49	3 3	...	4 32	5 45	7 30	†8 22	10 46	...	...
Teignmouth ...	*10 55	12 59	3 13	...	4 42	5 55	7 40	8 38	10 55	...	...
Newton arr	11 7	1 12	3 25	...	4 52	6 7	7 52	†9 0	11 5	...	...
Newton dep	11 12	1 18	3 30	...	4 58	6 12	8 0	10 0	11 7	...	...
Torquay Junc.	...	...	..	...	...	...	...	...	...	...	...
Totnes ...	11 33	‡1 38	3 50	...	5 14	6 32	8 25	11‡40	11‡25	...	...
Brent	11 54	2 1	4 8	...	5 29	*6 54	8 46	12 10	11 39	...	...
Kingsbridge Rd.	12 4	2 9	4 11	...	5 33	7 3	8 55	12 20	11 43	...	...
Ivybridge ...	12 13	2 18	4 20	...	5 38	7 12	9 2	12§30	11 48	...	...
Cornwood ..	12 19	2 24	4 24	p.m.	6 43	7 18	9 8	12 38	11 52	...	...
Plympton ...	12 32	2 38	4 32	5 0	5 51	7 32	9 21	12 54	12 0	...	...
Laira	...	...	...	...	...	...	...	1 4	...	..	...
Mutley... ...	12 42	2 48	4 40	5 10	...	7 42	9 31	1 17	12 7	...	...
Plymouth arr.	12 50	2 58	4 45	5 16	6 0	7 50	9 40	1 25	12 10	...	...
Plymouth dep.	...	p.m. 3 15	...	This Train will be worked by the Pilot which assists Up 4.10 p.m. Train to Hemerdon, or an Engine will be sent out special from Plymouth.	p.m 6 10	p.m. 7 55	p.m. 11 0	p.m. 10 0	..	...	...
Devonport ...	...	*3 25	...		6 15	8 0	11 5	10 18	...	...	...
Saltash ...	...	3 35	...		†6 25	8 10	11 14	10 30	...	...	...
St. Germans ...	...	3 49	...		6 39	8 24	WEDNESDAYS ONLY	10§55	...	...	...
Menheniot ...	...	4 3	...		*6 54	8 38		11 15	...	...	...
Liskeard ...	...	4 13	...		7 4	†8 50		12§10	...	...	...
Doublebois ...	...	†4 23	...		7 14			12 40	...	...	...
Bodmin Road...	...	4 38	...		7 29	Goods		1 10	...	...	...
Lostwithiel ...	...	4 47	...		†7 38	p.m.		1 55	...	...	..
Par	...	5 0	...		7 50	10 40		2 25	...	...	...
St. Austell ...	...	5 14	...		8 3	11 15		2 55	...	...	...
Burngullow ...	...	5 20	...		††8 8	11 45		3 25	...	...	...
Grampound Rd.	...	*5 32	...		†8 19	12 15		4 0	...	...	...
Truro .. arr.	...	††5 49	...		8 36	12 45		4 25	.	..	..
Truro .. dep.	...	5 58	...		8 45	...	..	MIXED GOODS.	..	...	...
Perranwell ...	...	6 8	...		8 55	...	...		...	...	...
Penryn ...	...	6 18	...		9 5	...	...		...	...	...
Falmouth arr.	...	6 28	...		9 15	...	...		...	...	...
Truro dep.	...	5 55	...	...	8 43	...	Morn.	a.m. ‡7 15	..	...	..
Newham ...	...	...	...	...	...	...	...	...	...	...	...
Chacewater ...	...	†6 8	...	...	8 58	...	...	7 40	...	...	...
Scorrier Gate...	...	6 14	...	...	9 4	...	...	§7 50	...	...	..
Redruth ...	...	6 22	...	...	9 12	...	...	8 5	...	...	...
Carn Brea Yard	...	...	...	...	...	...	...	...	...	...	...
Carn Brea ...	...	6 28	...	...	9 18	...	...	8 20	...	...	...
Camborne .	...	6 35	...	...	9 25	...	...	†8 49	...	...	...
Gwinear Road	...	6 42	...	...	9 33	...	...	§8 59	...	...	...
Hayle ..	...	*6 51	...	...	9 41	...	...	9 20	...	...	...
St. Ives Road	...	6 57	...	...	9 47	...	...	9 30	...	...	...
Marazion Road	...	7 6	...	...	9 57	...	...	†10 6	...	...	...
Penzance arr.	.	7 12	...	...	10 4	...	:	10 15	..	...	...

F A Pilot Engine must assist (No. 18) Down Good Train to Rattery. The Pilot Engine will return on the Up Line to Totnes, and then take a Goods Train from Totnes to Newton.

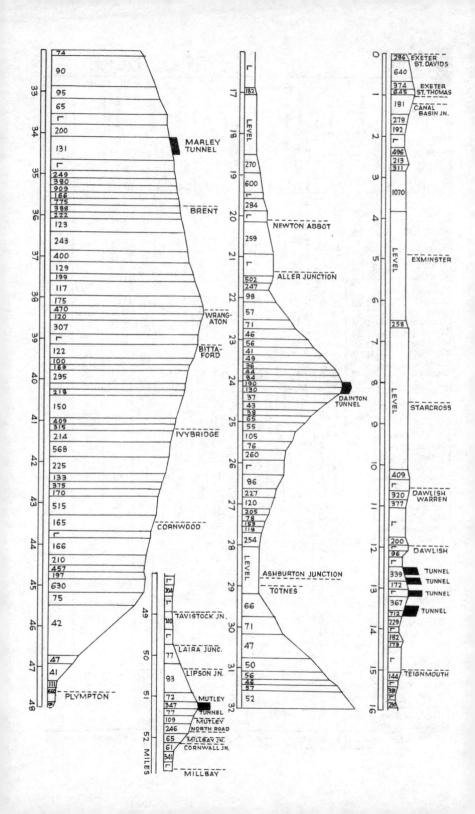